CW00644534

FLY DRESSING AND SOME TACKLE-MAKING

FLY DRESSING
AND
SOME TACKLE-MAKING

Written and Illustrated
By **W. E. (BILL) DAVIES**

PAPERFRONTS
ELLIOT RIGHT WAY BOOKS
KINGSWOOD SURREY U.K.

Made and Printed in Great Britain by Hunt Barnard Ltd., Aylesbury, Bucks.

Acknowledgement

I desire here to thank the Editors of the following magazines for permission to use quotations from articles of mine that have appeared in *Trout and Salmon, Stream and Field in Ireland.*

This book is for seven very good amateur fly-dressing friends of mine: Mrs. Barbara Taylor, George Armit, Jim Warne, Ron Glass, Keith Hall, Ray Chilvers and Ron Tomkins.

CONTENTS

TOOLS OF THE TRADE

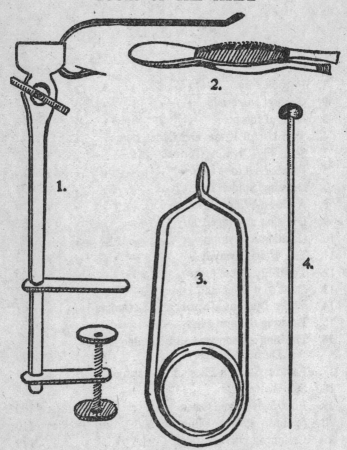

Fly-dressing Tools

1. Type of fly-vice that will take large hooks as well as the smallest
2. Tweezers   3. Pliers   4. Hat-pins

I

INTRODUCTORY

No matter how rapid the advance of technology during the next twenty-five years or so it is a fairly safe bet that the fabricating of flies for fishing will still be by hand.

Fly-dressing is a personal matter and the cold impersonal touch of a machine would do much to wreck the romantic halo which has surrounded the art for the past 2,000 years. Research has proved that artificial flies have been in use that period of time. Of course, it is possible that someone, some day will invent a robot capable of dressing flies, even the most complicated and resplendent salmon fly or the most delicate dry fly.

Be that as it may, in this age we have to rely on our hands, and personally I would not have it otherwise. It is always an added pleasure to take a wary trout, agile sea-trout or weighty salmon on a fly of one's own making.

The dressing of artificial flies, however, still remains a mystery to many ardent fishermen. Why it remains so is, indeed, the greatest mystery for flies are simple to construct, requiring only a few tools, some feathers, silk and tinsel, together with a few spare minutes of your time. Don't mistakenly think that it takes years to gain the necessary experience to dress a fly. Chances are the first fly you attempt will surprise you in its appearance and in its ability to take fish.

I suggest there are few anglers who go through a season without at least once wishing they could dress their own flies. The essentials are few, being a vice, pair of small sharp-pointed scissors, two pairs of fly-tier's pliers, tweezers, a small hat-pin, a piece of fly-tier's wax and a bottle of fly-tier's varnish. In respect of the vice, it is always best to purchase one that will take both trout and salmon hooks, otherwise you will have to have two.

As to materials, they include feathers, wool, fur, tying and floss silks and tinsels of various kinds and gauges. A game-keeper is a useful friend to have, as many of the birds he classes as vermin provide excellent feathers. Likewise he is a wise man who cultivates the friendship of poultry keepers.

There are, of course, a few firms in this country who specialize in catering for the wants of the amateur fly-dresser and all the mentioned tools and an assortment of materials are included in the fly-dressing kits that are on the market. Such a kit is ideal for any beginner of fly-dressing to own. A present I received from my parents many years ago was a kit purchased from Veniards of Thornton Heath, Surrey. The materials were long since exhausted but the tools are still in constant use.

The main thing in fly-dressing is to start with simple patterns first, graduating from trout to sea-trout and from there to salmon, putting in a little practice whenever possible. The best type of trout fly to commence with is a spider or hackle fly. Many anglers today fail to realize that the spider fly will take fish (*Salmonidaes*) all through the season. I know a winged dry fly for trout looks pretty as it dances over the wavelets, but we must not overlook the one thing for which the fly is made.

For instance, I have yet to hear of a trout stream where the March Brown, dressed spider fashion, does not find favour with both the angler and the trout.

Of course any instructor attempting to teach the technique of an art – and fly-dressing is an art – through the medium of the written word, must necessarily confine himself to a general method that will fit the average person. Explanation of each step in the work can be fully detailed, but these details must follow a concise pattern that makes no allowance for differences of personality or of adaptability. To do otherwise would merely mire the beginner down in a morass of technicalities that would probably cause him to give up in disgust.

After the beginner has dressed a few flies, he or she will

automatically begin developing a technique of their own and that is the ultimate goal of every instructor. When that point is reached and the beginner is striking out for himself, the instructor can lay down his pen.

However, since the first edition of this book was published there have been many changes in the fly dressing and fly fishing worlds and also in some materials and feathers used in the making of flies.

A few years ago the importing of jungle cock feathers from India was banned due to the near extinction of this beautiful bird, so alternatives had to be found as many salmon, sea trout and some trout patterns have jungle cock cheeks. I have devoted a small chapter on how to create such substitutes. Where a dressing includes jungle cock, don't be afraid to use a substitute for I have proved time and again, the fish don't mind.

Plastic raffia is now used for some patterns. More Rainbow trout are being "planted" in lakes and reservoirs than ever before with the result that many new patterns have appeared, a number of which I shall deal with in this enlarged edition.

2

GENERAL MATERIALS

OVER the years dressers of flies both professional and amateur have experimented with materials until today we have a list of what are undoubtedly the best possible for the job they have to do. Fly-fishermen the world over should be grateful to those individuals who spent hours over experiments with this and that material. They are the unsung heroes of the art.

Hackles are an important part of every fly. A good hackle enhances the luring qualities of the dresser's creation while a badly selected hackle destroys the illusion so far as the fish is concerned, that of imitating a natural insect. Bearing this in mind great care should be exercised when selecting feathers. For the present we will deal with trout-flies as the majority of hackles on these are natural while salmon and sea-trout are mostly dyed in various colours.

For wet trout-flies I believe that hen-hackles are best, they are soft and are not so buoyant as cock-hackles therefore they assist in sinking the fly. Hackles from wild birds are also used in the fabrication of a number of flies and the birds mostly in demand are starling, thrush, rook, moorhen, wild duck (teal and mallard), golden pheasant, common pheasant, partridge, woodcock, snipe, peacock, jay and grouse. Of course there are a host of others but the ones mentioned are in most common use.

Useful Feathers   *Illustration Key*

1. Jungle Cock
2. Mallard Drake blue feather
3. Teal Drake
4. Mallard Hen breast feather
5. Snipe hackle
6. Brown Partridge hackle
7. Golden Pheasant tippett
8. Guinea-Fowl hackle
9. Grouse hackle

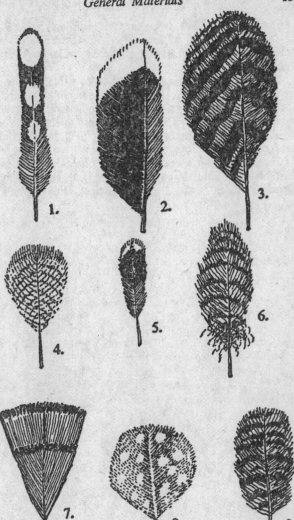

1. 2. 3.
4. 5. 6.
7. 8. 9.

For dry trout-flies two-year-old cock-hackles are considered best, being much stiffer in texture and better coloured than feathers from cockerels under or over that age.

The hackle is usually obtained from a feather near the head of the bird. From the nape of the neck downwards the feathers become larger and more webb (soft fibres) than those near the head. The small feathers at the back of the head are ideal for constructing spent flies and for hackles on fresh-water shrimps.

Other places on a cockerel where one can obtain hackle feathers are: Shoulders (spade-shaped), the back (long and slender hackles), and tail (Spey hackles). Only in a few flies

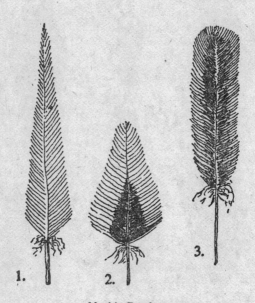

Hackle Feathers

1. Cock hackle   2 and 3. Hen hackles

are these particular hackles used so for the time being the amateur need only concern himself with neck hackle feathers.

Hackles from the neck of a hen are shaped much differently. Whereas those from a cockerel are sharp pointed and tapered in general shape, the ones from a hen are rounded and much more fluffy in appearance.

Breeds of poultry which provide excellent materials include Light Sussex, White Leghorn, Plymouth Rock, Black Leghorn, Rhode Island Red, Andalusian and Buff Wyandotte. Guinea-fowl feathers are not used much in trout-flies, but are used extensively in salmon-flies.

Wings

Most of the birds already mentioned, both wild and domesticated, provide the feathers from which the fly-dresser creates wings and those anglers who have pet budgerigars have a ready source of coloured feathers. For instance from the moulted wings of my yellow budgerigars I make wings for Yellow Sally flies and the breast and hackle feathers provide the materials for certain nymphs. A neighbour has a pair of white 'budgies' and the moulted tail feathers of these are excellent for the wings of the Coachman fly. The feathers from grey, blue and green budgerigars are all good. However, the making of trout-fly wings will be dealt with in a subsequent chapter.

Bodies

A great many different kinds of materials for fly bodies are used and these include: Wool dyed in varying colours, seals wool the same, fur from such animals as hares, rabbits, squirrels, fox and mole; quill, tying silk, floss silk, herl from feathers, raffia, chenille and tinsel. The last named is usually gold or silver and is used extensively in most flies whether trout, sea-trout or salmon. It is usually the flash of the tinsel which attracts the fish in the first instance.

Tails

These are usually made of two or three fibres from a feather. In dry flies the tail is an important part as it helps materially in balancing the fly as it rides on the surface of the water. Best tails for dry flies are made with fibres from a cockerel's hackle that has been taken from near the back of the head. Such a feather is both good in colour and stiff in texture.

Keeping Feathers

Moths like feathers so the wise fly-dresser takes precautions against raids by these winged terrors which can destroy a collection of valuable feathers in a very short time. Small cellophane packets are cheap enough these days and the beginner at fly-dressing obtains a number of such containers, sorts his flies, puts them in the packets and labels them so that they are easy to locate. In each packet it is wise to put a few crystals of paradiclorate of benzine, these will prevent any moths getting in should the packet have been left open.

Of course if one is handy with tools it is a fairly easy matter to make a cabinet to house the whole of the fly-dressing equipment.

First Aid for Feathers

Occasionally feathers will get out of shape, but there is a simple remedy for this. All that is required is a kettle containing boiling water that is sending out clouds of steam. With a pair of tweezers hold the feathers, one at a time, in the steam for five or ten seconds, then place each feather on a flat surface, put a sheet of paper on top and a couple of weighty books on top of the paper and in about half an hour the twisted feathers will have assumed their original shape.

Drying Rack for Flies

I had not been dressing flies long before I realized the need for a rack to put the finished flies on to dry. All one needs to make this useful adjunct to the kit is a couple of pieces of wood or hardboard, some stainless steel wire and a drill. Make the holes for the wire a shade smaller than the wire so that you get a tight fit. The sketch gives the general idea and the article will take about one hour to make.

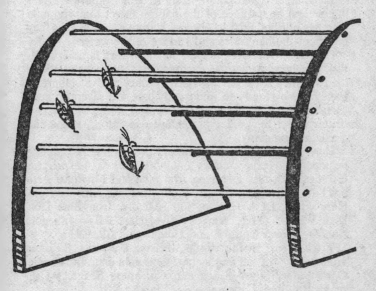

Drying rack for flies

3

NATURAL INSECTS

A LITTLE knowledge of natural insects and what they look like is of great help to the fly-dresser. It has been proved that trout on occasions can be the most selective of feeders, distinguishing between one insect and another. The successful angler-cum-fly-dresser is usually one who has taken the trouble to acquaint himself with the various water insects in the area he operates. With such knowledge his artificial creations are more likely to come somewhere near the general appearance of the natural insect than the man who has not bothered to observe Nature's creations as they flit about the banksides and surface of the water.

Of course there are quite a number of very famous trout-flies that have no natural counterparts. Such flies as Wickham's Fancy, Coachman, Cairn's Fancy and Swinburne's Fancy come readily to mind and there are several others. They all score in that while not representing any one particular insect they are representative in colour, shape and size of a good many.

Here then is a list which should prove of some value to beginner and expert alike: *Scientific name, Ephemeridae* includes such flies as olives, iron blue and Mayflies. Artificial flies to represent this group includes Blue Upright, Hare's Ear, Dark Hackle, Tup, Mayfly, Iron Blue Dun, Blue Winged Olive, Winged Olive, Hare's Ear with gold ribbing, Brown Upright, and Greenwell's Glory.

Trichoptera: In this group we have the sedge flies and grannoms. Artificial flies include Grannom male and female, Dark Sedge, Silver Sedge and Cinnamon Sedge, Welshman's Button or Caperer.

Diptera: Includes cranefly (daddy-longlegs), gnats, and midges. Artificials for this group include Black Gnat, Brown

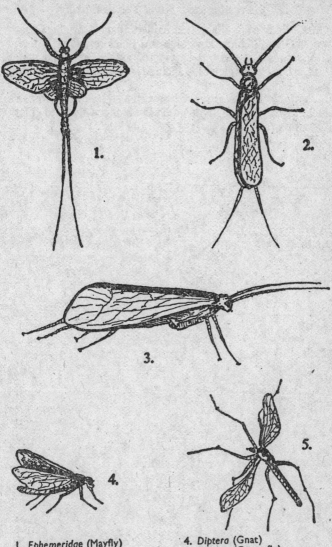

1. *Ephemeridae* (Mayfly)
2. *Perlidae* (Stone-fly)
3. *Trichoptera* (Caddis-fly)
4. *Diptera* (Gnat)
5. *Diptera* (Crane-fly)

Gnat, Black Midge, Knotted Midge, Black Upright, Green-well's Glory, Yellow Partridge and Black and Gold.

Sialidae: The various species of alder flies come under this group. Artificial flies include Alder, Dark Alder and Silver Alder.

Perlidae: In this group we have the stone-flies. Artificials include Stone-fly, Light and Dark Stone-fly and Dark Greenwell's Glory.

4

TWO USEFUL KNOTS AND OTHER ITEMS

THERE are two knots the fly-dresser should know. First is the HALF-HITCH which is used largely throughout the dressing of a fly, whether it be for trout, sea-trout or salmon. There is no need for me to go into details in respect of this simple knot, as a glance at the sketch will show how easy it is to do.

The second is the WHIP-FINISH, which looks tricky to tie, but is not, once you understand that its purpose is merely to bury the end of the winding under itself. The beauty of the knot lies in the fact that the head of a fly can be tapered and as a result the finished job looks much neater.

Some fly-dressers don't bother with the whip-finish, but tie in at the head two, three or more half-hitches on top of each other. A head finished in this way does not look nice, it is bulky and far from being neat. Whether a fish can tell

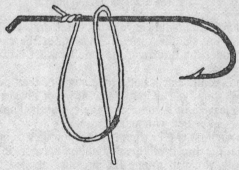

Half-Hitch Knot

the difference I do not know, but a craftsman who takes a pride in his work likes to turn out a good article, so my advice is always use the whip-finish.

Here is the way to finish off the head of a fly. Hold the end of the thread in the left hand (assuming you are right-handed) and form a loop in the thread with the middle and fore-fingers of the right, so that the thread crosses itself. Lay the thread you are holding in your left hand parallel with the shank of the hook and hold it there while, by rolling the fingers of your right hand inside the loop, you pass four or five turns of thread over the head of the fly. The idea is to wind the thread over itself and then, by pulling

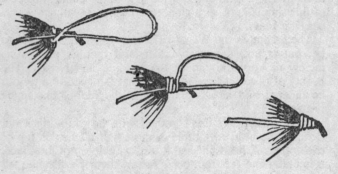

Three Steps to Whip-Finish

the end you are holding in your left hand, draw the last loop tight and cut off the surplus. This buries the end of the thread under the turns and the tie-off cannot possibly fray or come loose.

Sounds complicated, but a little study of the three drawings will show you that it isn't. However always bear in mind to leave a little room near the eye of the hook so that the knot can be tied without any trouble.

With the first two or three 'whips' you tie it is quite possible that the thread will break, but don't give up in despair. Gradually you will attune the pressure applied and you should have no further trouble.

Preparing Tinsel

When using flat tinsel for ribbing or making bodies it is always advisable to cut the end to be tied in on the hook shank into the shape of a wedge. By doing this the tinsel shapes better to the shank and there is no unsightly bulge.

Thoughts on Hooks

When you purchase hooks (eyed) in various sizes be sure they come from a reputable firm. Cheap hooks are false economy and should be avoided. For wet flies (trout) the eyes are usually down-turned and for dry flies, up-turned. With salmon one can get hooks with either up-turned or down-turned eyes.

With dry-fly hooks it is always best to check and see that they have been constructed of fine gauge wire, hooks made of such assist materially in keeping the fly afloat. Remember the finished fly has to be balanced, in most cases, on hackle and tail. A heavy hook acts against such a balance being achieved.

Wax

For years I used solid wax for treating tying silk so that it grips the shank of the hook and makes it waterproof, but about ten years ago a friend gave me a recipe for making liquid wax; here it is: Bring a saucepan of water to the boil and when boiling put in a smaller sized pan into which has been put some resin and turpentine. A quarter of a pound of resin to four dessert table-spoonfuls of turpentine makes enough to last for years. Mine is kept in a glass jar with screw-top.

To make solid wax is just as simple. A quarter of a pound of resin (white or amber) is put into a saucepan together with a dessert spoonful of neatsfoot oil. Heat over a gas-stove and when melted pour into another pan containing warm water. As soon as the wax is cool enough to handle start kneading it with both hands until it takes on the consistency of sticky toffee. Rolled into balls it can be kept in a glass jar that has been half-filled with water. After use the wax should be returned to the water to keep it pliable.

Occasionally in warm weather it will be found that this type of wax will adhere to the fingers. A cloth upon which has been placed some methylated spirit will soon remove it.

Varnish

For the heads of trout and sea-trout flies a good varnish (brown in colour) can be made from shellack and methylated spirit. A pound-size glass jam-jar is three-parts filled with shellack and then topped off with methylated spirit. After three days the mixture is stirred a few times and in another couple of days it is ready for use.

This varnish is also useful when making splices in lines.

5

SOME FLY-DRESSING TERMS

Like most crafts and arts there are various terms used in the fabricating of flies. For instance a fly might have a cocked wing, down wing, hair wing, rolled wing, etc. The newcomer will come across such terms early in his career and may well wonder what they mean. Here are some of the principle ones.

Down Wing: This means that the wings lie flat along the body and is generally used to imitate stone-flies and caddis-flies.

Rolled Wings: These are used for quite a number of flies and simply means that a section of a primary or secondary feather has been taken and rolled between thumb and fore-finger to the shape of a wing.

Cocked Wings: Used when referring to the wings of a dry fly, which are upright like those of the natural insect.

Spent Wings: refer to the use of hackle tips to represent a fly that has laid its eggs on the surface of the water and is floating, dead or dying, downstream.

Fan Wings: Usually applied when speaking of dry May-flies.

Hair Wings: Are so termed when the wing part of the fly has been constructed of hair from animals.

We next come to bodies and here again there are a few terms which indicate the major make-up of the body.

Tinsel Body: When it is entirely composed of silver or gold tinsel. This type of body also includes the material lurex.

Palmered Body: Indicates that a small hackle feather has

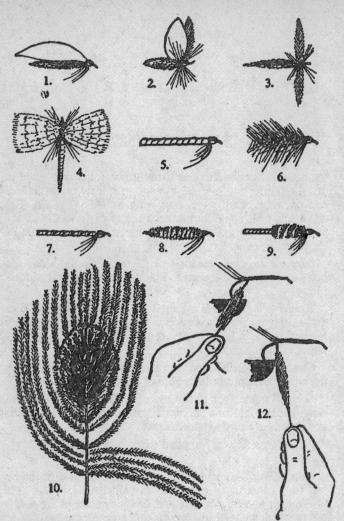

Illustration Key

1. Down wing
2. Upright wing
3. Spent wing
4. Fan wing
5. Tinsel body
6. Palmer body
7. Quill body
8. Peacock herl body
9. Tinsel and wool body
10. Peacock Feather showing herl strands
11. Preparing 'dubbing'
12. 'Dubbing' ready to wind

been wound round the body, such as one finds in the various palmer type of flies and Wickham's Fancy, etc.

Quill Body: Mostly used on small flies to show off the insect's segmented body. The material is obtained from the quill of a feather. Actually it is the skin which covers the pith inside the quill.

Sectional Body: Means that the fly has a body construction of different colours or materials. The term is generally used when referring to certain sea-trout and salmon-flies.

Herl Body: Quite a large number of trout-flies have this type of body. Peacock herl is used for a large number of flies such as the Coachman, Red Tag, Coch-y-Bondhu, etc. Herl is a filament from a feather, usually a primary. Cock pheasant, hen pheasant and heron herl is used in the making of a number of small trout-flies. The hairlike strands give such a body translucency when in the water.

Wool Body: It would be hard to say with any degree of accuracy how many flies, trout, sea-trout and salmon have wool bodies for there are many hundreds. The wool used is of different sorts, but the one most in use today is what is known as seal's wool and this can be had dyed in all sorts of basic colours and tints. In recent years there has come on to the market a wool that is fluorescent and many claims have been put forward as to its luring capabilities by angling-writers who have given it exhaustive tests. Two years ago I used flies with such bodies to the exclusion of all other types and at the end of the season I had caught fourteen more trout than the previous season, so perhaps there may be something in the claims made.

With all bodies made of wool or fur the material has to be spun on to the thread, an operation which is quite easy to perform. In fly-dressing circles it is usually called 'Dubbing'. Here is how it is done. The tying thread is well waxed, and for this job liquid wax is much better, a little seal's wool or fur is pressed on to the thread with the right thumb and forefinger while the thread is held taut with the thumb and forefinger of the other hand. Then start twisting the thread and material together with the thumb and forefinger of the right hand. In a few seconds it will take on the form of yarn and can then be wound on to the shank of the hook.

To make bodies with other like materials necessitates the same process.

6

PARTS OF A TROUT FLY

BEFORE we get down to the real job of dressing a trout-fly it might be a good idea to explain the various parts that go to make up the whole. The fly illustrated is that of a wet pattern for trout. Salmon-flies are a little more intricate in design so will be dealt with separately, because before one can properly dress these a thorough apprenticeship must have been made on smaller flies. On the face of it one would assume that larger flies would be much easier to handle; they are, but only after much practice and the finest I can suggest is that of dressing trout-flies.

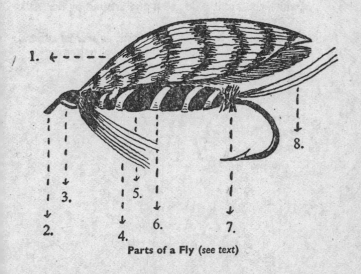

Parts of a Fly (see text)

Here then are the essential parts of a fly:

1. Wings. In a dry fly they would be upright, or if a spider, the hackle which then becomes the wings would be at right-angles to the shank, something like the spokes of a wheel.

2. Eye of hook. A dry fly would have the eye up-turned.

3. Head of fly, tapered off as only the whip-finish can give.

4. Hackle. In a dry fly it would be at right-angles to the shank and be made from a cock's hackle feather. The hackle on a wet pattern is usually made from a hen hackle as it is much softer and aids sinking.

5. Floss body. Body materials are many and varied.

6. Tinsel ribbing which give flash to fly. Main colours used are gold and silver.

7. Tag. This is used in some patterns to give an impression of egg-sacs. The Grannom is such a fly in which the sac is pale green and created by floss silk or dyed ostrich herl.

8. Tail. This is usually made of fibres from feathers, stiff for dry-flies, not so stiff for wet patterns.

7

DRESSING A SPIDER DRY FLY

THE preliminaries completed let us get down to the job of creating a dry spider fly for trout. Spider patterns, dry or wet, are the most simple of all flies to make. The one we are about to embark upon is for practice only.

The tools are on the table and the vice is clamped to the edge of the table with a No. 12, up-turned eye fastened between the jaws.

A foot-length piece of tying silk thread is waxed and fastened by our old friend the half-hitch midway on the shank and wound back to near the hook bend. This makes a firm foundation for the body of the fly and prevents it slipping round. Three fibres from a cock's-hackle feather, any colour will do as this is just for practice, are tied in with a half-hitch. Next a couple of peacock-herl strands are put in with the half-hitch, the hackle pliers are clipped to the other ends and the herl is wound round the shank to near the eye. A half-hitch fastens the herl and the surplus is cut off. The fly should now look like sketch No. 3.

The hackle is fastened in *butt* first with a half-hitch; pliers are clipped to the tip and the feather is wound round three times. The silk thread is wound twice between the hackle fibres which brings it to near the eye. Surplus hackle is cut off, whip-finish knot is made and the fly should look like drawing No. 6.

At least two dozen practice flies should be made before attempting to make an actual fly for fishing with. Of course the first half a dozen efforts may be poor in appearance; however with plenty of serious practice your work will get better until you arrive at the stage when you can really get down to the job of dressing some of your favourite patterns on smaller hooks.

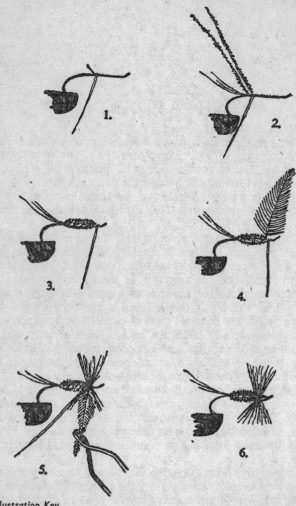

Illustration Key

1. Thread is fastened to hook shank
2. Tail and peacock herl is tied in
3. Body is made
4. Hackle is put on
5. Hackle being wound on
6. The completed fly

If the No. 12 hook looks too small for practising on use a bigger one by all means, until you have more experience.

To make a wet spider fly the hackle feather is usually taken from the neck of a hen bird. With quite a number of artificial flies the hackles are dyed to the general colour of the insect one is trying to imitate.

A close study of the sketches will help considerably in the making of that all important first fly.

8

A DOWN-WINGED PATTERN

DOWN-WINGED patterns are useful throughout the whole season and are particularly deadly in the evening when the water is fining down after a spate. However, a little different technique is involved as the drawings illustrate.

In No. 1 a tail has been tied in, a wool body is put on and several fibres of a hen-hackle feather is tied in as per sketch No. 3.

We now come to the wings and any soft-textured feather such as jay, blackbird, thrush, waterhen, etc., is ideal providing it conforms to the general colouration of the fly we are imitating. But as in our previous chapter on a hackle dry fly this is only for practice. A section of the selected feather is cut, see sketches Nos. 4 and 5, and folded evenly as drawing No. 6. The folded fibres are trimmed and tied in as per No. 7, the surplus is trimmed off and the finished fly appears as No. 8.

Scores of wet-fly patterns have wings composed in this manner. To name only a few we have the famous Greenwell's Glory, March Brown, Olive Quill, Iron Blue Dun, Rough Olive, Blue Dun, Woodcock and Hare's Ear, etc.

Make half a dozen down-wings for practice. No doubt you will be getting a little bored by my continual use of the word 'Practice' but I know no other way of becoming a flydresser. The more time spent in practice the quicker one turns out a well-dressed fly.

By now your fingers will be more supple and the half-hitch and whip-finish knots should have been mastered together with putting in of tails and hackles. Of course you will not be turning out a fly every few minutes, but experience should enable you to do that within a very short time.

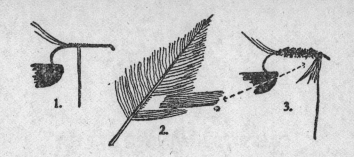

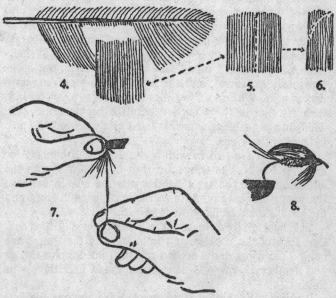

Illustration Key

1. Hook is placed in vice and tail tied in
2. A dozen fibres are taken from hackle feather and tied in
3. A section of a primary feather is cut out
4. Section with dotted line to be folded
5. The folded section with dotted line shows where to trim
6. How to hold the wings when tying in
7. Tying in the hackle
8. The finished fly

9

DRESSING A WINGED DRY FLY

DURING the months of May, June, July, August and
September myriads of insects are flitting about the surface of the water and the winged dry fly really comes into
its own, so our next practice fly will be of that type.

For the wings one has to use sections from two separate
feathers, see drawing No. 1 and 2 on page 37. A half-
hitch ties in the silk thread, the tail and body is put on as
previously explained, and the job of putting on the wings
comes next. With most wet flies the wings are put on last,
with dry flies of the winged variety the hackle comes last.
This change enables the hackle to sit nicely behind and also
in front of the wings.

The wings are tied in with a couple of half-hitches, see
drawing No. 5. The wings are then held upright with the
left hand while the right hand winds the silk in between
the wings, finishing off with a couple of turns in front and
the result should be like drawing No. 6.

The hackle is put in and the pliers clipped to the end.
One turn of the hackle is made in front of the wings, one
behind the wings and a second one in front. Surplus thread
and feather is cut off, whip-finish made and the fly is
finished.

It might take three or four practice flies before one gets
the knack of 'cocking' the wings and putting on the hackle.

A Winged Dry Fly	Illustration Key
1. Two primary feathers section taken for wings	5. Wings tied on
2. The sections together	6. Wings are cocked
3. Silk thread tied in	7. Hackle put in
4. Tail and body put on	8. The finished fly

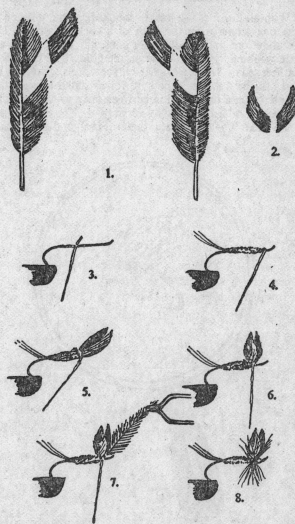

With all dry flies the hackle should be extra stiff and the best ones come from the nape of a cockerel's neck. They are about one and a half inches long, stiff, and there is very little webbing (softness) between the fibres. The best hackle feathers come from two-year-old cockerels. Similarly the fibres of the tail should be stiff, for as stated in a previous chapter such a combination between tail and hackle aids in balancing and keeping the fly afloat.

To make 'floatability' still better it is a good idea to singe

A Dry Fly showing 'feet' under magnifying glass

the lower hackle with the lighted end of a cigarette. With this treatment the ends of the fibres develop 'feet'. See sketch on page 38.

Hook sizes for the most popular dry flies will be given in the chapter devoted to trout patterns and dressings.

10

CREATING A NYMPH

No book on fly-dressing would be complete without a mention of nymphs. Throughout the whole season trout feed on nymphs. However, it was not until exhaustive studies had been carried out by G. E. M. Skues between 1880 and 1900 that fly-dressers started to create artificials.

Prior to that it had been practised by a few observant anglers who noticed that when a wet fly became little more than a bare hook, trout would strike repeatedly at it. Why? was the question often asked. This sort of thing had been going on for years and those anglers who discovered the secret kept it to themselves. Then along came Skues and he tore aside for ever the cloak of mystery of why trout on certain occasions liked very little dressing on the hooks. Such flies had the appearance of nymphs or larvae of the under-water insects upon which they fed. Skues and others continued their studies and it was not long before anglers realized the artificial nymph had come to stay.

Of course when you stop to think about the matter it becomes obvious that when there are no flies hatching trout must be feeding on something, for like YOU or I trout have to eat to live. Therefore he is a wise angler who includes in his box or book a few patterns of these immature insects.

In sketch No. 1 a short tail has been tied in. In the next drawing a section of a blackbird's (cock) primary feather is put on and No. 3 sees the formation of the body by spinning a little wool or fur on to the well-waxed thread. The body is completed in No. 4. In the following sketch the blackbird-feather section is brought over to near the head, tied in and the surplus cut off. This forms the wing case.

A small hackle feather is put on as in sketch No. 5 and

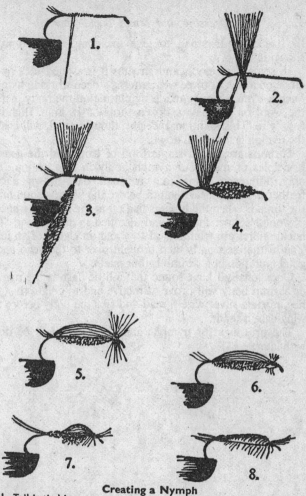

Creating a Nymph

1. Tail is tied in
2. Section of a blackbird (cock) primary feather is fixed
3. Wool for body is spun on thread
4. Body completed
5. The feather section is brought to the head and hackle is put on
6. Hackle is trimmed and nymph is complete
7. Another form of nymph   8. Shrimp

the hackle is trimmed to give the completed nymph as shown in No. 6.

In some deep pools and streams it is a good idea to include on a cast of three wet patterns a deep working nymph. Such a nymph can be made by putting on the body, before the wool or fur, half a dozen turns of 10 amp. (lighting) fuse wire. This additional weight, though small, will ensure the nymph getting well down.

Shrimps are also a staple food of trout and the general principles of making a nymph apply in its creation. The only difference being that a small dark-brown hackle feather is tied in near the tail before the wool is spun on to the thread. When the body is tied off at the head, the hackle is wound palmer fashion and also tied in at the head. The hackle fibres are trimmed off to about an eighth of an inch. The feather section is then brought over to the head and a good imitation of a shrimp is thus made.

Occasionally I have found that a little flash in the nymph or shrimp body will prove attractive and to create this one ties in some silver wire thread and ribs the body before the wing-case is made.

The dressings for nymphs and hook sizes will be dealt with later.

11

THE WINGED MAYFLY

Tᴴɪs is the last of the practice flies we shall be dressing until we reach the section dealing with sea-trout and salmon-fly making.

When I was a boy winged dry Mayflies had the tail and part of the body constructed separately. A fly so made was known as a detached or offset body fly. The detached portion was made of cork, raffia, quill or rubber. Today with very few exceptions, Mayflies are dressed on fine wire, long-shanked hooks; they look just as good and trout don't seem to mind the change in dressing.

The long-shanked hook type are much easier to dress in that the fly is dealt with as a whole. In the old method the tail and part of the long, tapering body was constructed first and then attached to the shank of the hook. This made the job of dressing a Mayfly take nearly twice as long. I have no doubt that it was this time factor which led to the change-over.

About fifty years ago most rivers and lakes throughout the country had their Mayfly hatches, but today only a small percentage of our waters give birth to this most beautiful of water-side flies. However, more and more anglers are visiting Ireland for trout fishing and as this particular country has hatches on most of its rivers and lakes I have devoted a chapter to its dressing.

The fly is known as a fan-wing; the feathers for this come from the breast of a mallard duck and are a lovely shade of grey.

In drawing No. 1 three strands of a cock pheasant's tail have been tied in and No. 2 shows the feathers prepared ready. In sketch No. 3 a gold-coloured body made of raffia with a ribbing of gold wire has been made and one wing

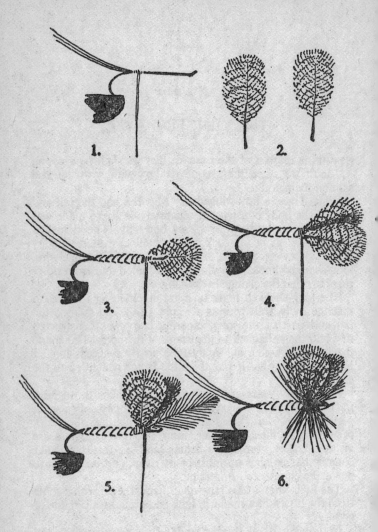

1. Long tail put on
2. Small breast feathers of
   Mallard Duck
3. Body and wing tied
4. Second wing put on
5. Wings upright and hackle
   tied in
6. Finished fly

put on. In the next drawing both wings are in and No. 5 sees them 'cocked' and the hackle (dyed yellow) is tied in. In No. 6 we have the finished fly.

There are several different dressings of the winged (dry) Mayfly, but the one above takes some beating.

A friend of mine, Jack Stack of Westport, Ireland, a skilled amateur fly-dresser and one-time world champion trout angler, has the wings of the Mayfly he dresses a pale olive green in colour while the hackle of its wet counterpart is made from a pale yellow dyed French partridge hackle feather.

For the spent fly the mallard feathers give place to dyed yellow hackle points as per illustration No. 3 in Chapter 5.

During the height of a Mayfly hatch a heavy shower of rain or a heavy wind might batter the flies on to the surface of the water and drown them before they have a chance to mate and lay their eggs. In such an event a good dressing for a wet Mayfly is body and tail as already illustrated, but instead of wings we have a pale olive green hackle put on first and then a pale yellow (dyed) French partridge hackle tied in.

This wet fly dressing is also productive during an end of a hatch period, and occasionally when the hatch is just beginning.

A friend of mine has had considerable success with the following dressing: Tail is three fibres of a cock pheasant's tail feather, body is made of white floss silk ribbed with black tying silk thread, wings are mallard breast feathers dyed pale brown and hackle is deep yellow.

12

TROUT-FLY DRESSINGS

BEFORE this chapter was planned I carried out a research among a number of professional dressers in England, Scotland, Wales and Ireland, believing that by so doing one could get a rough idea as to what patterns were in greatest demand. Of the dressers approached more than 80 per cent were in agreement that they had orders for the March Brown far in excess of any other pattern, so this fly takes pride of place.

Wet (spider) hackle flies will be dealt with first, winged wet second, next dry-fly spiders and winged dry flies last.

Hook sizes (old numbers) are given at the end of each dressing.

MARCH BROWN (SPIDER) WET

Tail: Two fibres of a partridge feather taken from the back of the bird.
Body: Brown wool or fur ribbed with fine gold wire.
Hackle: Brown partridge feather from bird's back.
Hook: No. 14.

GREENWELL'S GLORY

Tail: Three fibres of a furnace hackle (colour of this feather is reddish brown with a black marking down the centre.
Body: Well-waxed yellow tying silk ribbed with fine gold wire.
Hackle: Furnace hackle from hen.
Hook: No. 14 or No. 16 for small streams and No. 10 or 12 for lake fishing.

IRON BLUE DUN

Tail: Two fibres of a Blue Andalusian cock's hackle.

Body: Blue-grey coloured fur with two turns of red silk next to the tail.
Hackle: A hackle feather from the inside of a snipe's wing.
Hook: No. 14 or 16.

SNIPE AND PURPLE

Body: Purple tying silk, shank of the hook wound twice.
Hackle: Snipe. Hook No. 14 or 16 for river fishing. No. 12 for lake work.

BLACK SPIDER

Body: Black fur or wool ribbed silver wire.
Hackle: Feather from the neck of a Black Leghorn.
Hook: No. 14 or 16 for streams. No. 12 lakes.

ORANGE PARTRIDGE

Body: Orange silk, ribbed with gold wire.
Hackle: Brown mottled feather from partridge's neck.
Hook: No. 14 or 16.

YELLOW PARTRIDGE

Body: Yellow silk, ribbed with fine gold wire.
Hackle: Grey barred feather from partridge's breast.
Hook: No. 14 or 16.

SPRING BLACK

Body: Purple silk, ribbed with magpie herl.
Hackle: Feather from an adult starling's neck.
Hook: No. 14 or 16.

DARK BLOA

Body: Claret tying silk.
Hackle: Black hen neck hackle.
Hook: No. 16.

RED SPINNER

Body: Red tying silk with dubbing of maroon wool, ribbed with fine gold wire.
Hackle: Rhode Island Red hen hackle feather.
Hook: No. 14 or 16.

Zulu

Tail: Red wool or red ibis feather fibres.
Body: Black floss silk, ribbed fine silver wire.
Hackle: Black hackle tied in at bend of hook and wound
palmer fashion.
Hook: No. 12 or 14.

Blue Zulu

Tail: Red wool or red ibis feather fibres.
Body: Blue floss silk, ribbed fine silver wire.
Hackle: Black hackle tied in at bend of hook and wound
palmer fashion.
Hook: No. 12 or 14.

Red Tag

Tail: Red wool one-16th of inch in length.
Body: Bronze peacock herl.
Hackle: From Rhode Island hen.
Hook: No. 12, 14 or 16.

Grouse and Yellow

Body: Yellow floss silk, ribbed fine gold wire.
Hackle: Grouse feather, well marked, from breast of bird.
Hook: No. 14 or 16.

Bracken Clock

Body: Bronze peacock herl, ribbed red tying silk.
Hackle: Feather from cock pheasant neck which is golden
brown in colour with black tips.
Hook: No. 14 or 16.

Priest

This is also a good grayling fly.

Tail: Red wool or fibres of red ibis feather.
Body: Flat silver tinsel, ribbed fine oval silver tinsel.
Hackle: Well marked feather of natural badger cock.
Hook: No. 14 or 16.

OLIVE DUN

   Tail: Three fibres from olive cock hackle.
   Body: Olive quill.
   Hackle: Blue dun hen.
   Hook: No. 14 or 16.

BLAE AND BLACK

   Tail: Four fibres of golden pheasant tippet.
   Body: Black seal's wool.
   Hackle: Black hen.
   Hook: No. 14 or 16.

BADGER AND GOLD

   This is also a good grayling fly.
   Body: Flat gold tinsel, ribbed fine gold wire.
   Hackle: Natural badger hen.
   Hook: No. 14 or 16.

Winged Wet Flies

MARCH BROWN

   Tail: Three brown partridge wing fibres.
   Body: Brown hare's fur, ribbed fine gold wire.
   Hackle: Brown partridge.
   Wings: Taken from brown partridge primary feather.
   Hook: No. 14 and 16. No. 10 and 12 for lakes.

GREENWELL'S GLORY

   Body: Well-waxed yellow tying silk, ribbed fine gold wire.
   Hackle: Light furnace cock.
   Wings: Hen blackbird wing feather taken from near the
   tip, and rolled.
   Hook: No. 14 and 16. No. 10 and 12 for lakes.

GOLD RIBBED HARE'S EAR

   Body: Brown hare's fur, ribbed fine gold wire or flat gold
   tinsel.
   Hackle: This is formed by picking out some of the fur
   fibres with a needle.

Wings: Taken from starling wing feather and rolled.
Hook: No. 14 or 16.

IRON BLUE DUN

Tail: Three fibres from iron blue hackle.
Body: Three turns of red tying silk next to tail, remainder
of body slate-grey fur.
Hackle: Iron blue.
Wings: From jay's wing feather.
Hook: No. 14 or 16 and No. 12 for lakes.

OLIVE DUN

Tail: Three fibres of light olive.
Body: Light olive quill.
Hackle: Olive dun.
Wings: Taken from snipe's wing feather and rolled.
Hook: No. 14, 16 or 18.

RED SPINNER

Tail: Three fibres from red cock's hackle.
Body: Red floss silk, ribbed fine gold wire.
Hackle: Red cock.
Wings: Hen blackbird and rolled.
Hook: No. 14 or 16. No. 12 for lakes.

WICKHAM'S FANCY

Tail: Three fibres of ginger-red cock hackle.
Body: Flat gold tinsel.
Hackle: Small ginger-red hackle tied in by tip next to tail
and wound to the shoulder.
Wings: From starling and rolled, or can be made by
taking a section from a left-wing feather and one from
a right-wing feather.
Hook: No. 14 or 16. No. 10 or 12 for lakes.

BLOODY BUTCHER

Tail: Red ibis or dyed feather.
Body: Flat silver tinsel, ribbed oval silver tinsel.

Wings: Section from blue feathers right and left wings of mallard drake.
Hackle: Red.
Hook: No. 14 or 16. No. 10 or 12 for lakes.

BUTCHER

Tail: Red ibis or dyed feather.
Body: Flat silver tinsel ribbed oval silver tinsel.
Hackle: Black hen.
Wings: Same as Bloody Butcher.
Hook: No. 14 or 16. No. 10 or 12 for lakes.

GOLDEN BUTCHER

Tail: Red ibis or dyed feather.
Body: Flat gold tinsel, ribbed oval gold tinsel.
Hackle: Usually black hen, but has been dressed with red hackle.
Wings: As before.
Hook: No. 14 or 16. No. 10 or 12 for lakes.

COACHMAN

Body: Bronze peacock herl.
Hackle: Brown.
Wings: White duck or any soft white feather that can be rolled.
Hook: No. 14 or 16. No. 12 for lakes.

YELLOW SALLY

Body: Bright yellow seal's wool or fur.
Hackle: Pale ginger.
Wings: Deep yellow dyed feather that can be rolled.
Hook: No. 14 or 16.

PETER ROSS

Tail: Four golden pheasant tippet fibres.
Body: First half starting from tail is flat silver tinsel, second half is red seal's wool ribbed fine oval tinsel.
Hackle: Black hen.
Wings: Teal, well-marked barred feather.
Hook: No. 14 or 16. No. 12 for lakes.

TEAL AND CLARET

Tail: Four fibres of golden pheasant tippet.
Body: Claret seal's wool, ribbed fine gold wire.
Hackle: Dyed claret hen.
Wings: Teal well-marked barred feather.
Hook: No. 14 or 16. No. 12 for lakes.

TEAL AND GREEN

Tail: Four fibres of golden pheasant tippet.
Body: Green seal's wool, ribbed fine gold wire.
Hackle: Black hen.
Wings: Teal barred feather.
Hook: No. 14 or 16. No. 12 for lakes.

TEAL AND SILVER

Tail: Four fibres of golden pheasant tippet.
Body: Flat silver tinsel, ribbed fine oval tinsel.
Hackle: Black hen.
Wings: Teal barred feather.
Hook: No. 14 or 16. No. 12 for lakes.

ALEXANDRA

Tail: Three tips of green peacock herl one-eighth of an inch long.
Body: Flat silver tinsel, ribbed final oval tinsel.
Hackle: Can be black or brown hen.
Wings: Six to eight short strands of green and bronze peacock herl and on each side of wing is placed a narrow piece of red ibis or dyed feather.
Hook: No. 14 or 16. No. 10 or 12 for lakes.

JUNGLE ALEXANDRA

Tail: Red ibis or dyed feather.
Body: As in Alexandra.
Hackle: As in Alexandra.
Wings: Six to eight short strands of green and bronze peacock herl, with small jungle cock feather on either side.
Hook: As in Alexandra.

GROUSE AND YELLOW

Tail: Four fibres of golden pheasant tippet.
Body: Yellow seal's wool, ribbed fine gold wire.
Hackle: Canary yellow hen.
Wings: From grouse primary feather.
Hook: No. 14 or 16. No. 10 or 12 for lakes.

GROUSE AND CLARET

Tail: Four or six fibres of golden pheasant tippet.
Body: Claret seal's wool, ribbed fine gold wire or fine oval gold tinsel.
Hackle: Black or furnace hackle feather.
Wings: From grouse primary feather.
Hook: No. 14 or 16. No. 10 or 12 for lakes.

MALLARD AND CLARET

Tail: Four fibres of golden pheasant tippet.
Body: Claret seal's wool, ribbed fine oval gold tinsel.
Hackle: Red.
Wings: Bronze mallard.
Hook: No. 14 or 16. No. 10 or 12 for lakes.

GRANNOM

Body: One turn of green floss silk at end of hook shank, remainder of body light brown hare's fur.
Hackle: Pale ginger.
Wings: Partridge wing feather rolled.
Hook: No. 14 or 16.

PROFESSOR

Tail: Three half-inch fibres of red ibis feather.
Body: Yellow floss silk, ribbed fine gold wire.
Hackle: Ginger.
Wings: Grey mallard from duck or drake.
Hook: No. 14 or 16. No. 10 or 12 for lakes.

WOODCOCK AND GOLD

Tail: Three fibres of golden pheasant tippet.
Body: Flat gold tinsel, ribbed gold wire.
Hackle: Furnace.
Wings: From wing feather of woodcock, rolled.
Hook: No. 14 or 16. No. 12 for lakes.

Woodcock and Yellow

Tail: Three fibres of golden pheasant tippet.
Body: Yellow seal's wool, ribbed oval gold tinsel.
Hackle: Furnace.
Wings: Woodcock wing feather, rolled.
Hook: No. 14 or 16. No. 12 for lakes.

Sand Fly

Body: Dark fur from hare's ear.
Hackle: Ginger.
Wings: Section from a landrail's wing feather, rolled.
Hook: No. 16.

Black Gnat

Body: Black ostrich herl.
Wings: Made from section of jackdaw's wing feather and rolled.
Hook: No. 16 or 18.

Hackle (Spider Dry Flies)

March Brown

Tail: Three brown partridge wing fibres.
Body: Brown hare's fur, ribbed fine gold wire.
Hackle: First make two turns of a red cock hackle and then put in a nice mottled hackle from the back of a partridge, and make a couple of turns so that it mixes with the red hackle.
Hook: No. 14 or 16.

Greenwell's Glory

Body: Yellow waxed silk, ribbed gold wire.
Hackle: Furnace cock.
Hook: No. 14 or 16. No. 10 or 12 for lakes.

Golden Palmer

Body: Gold floss silk, ribbed gold wire.
Hackle: Two red cock hackles are wound the full length of hook shank.
Hook: No. 10, 12 or 14.

RED PALMER

Body: Red seal's wool, ribbed gold wire.
Hackle: As in Golden Palmer.
Hook: As in Golden Palmer.

BLACK PALMER

Body: Black ostrich herl or seal's wool, ribbed silver wire.
Hackle: Two black hackles wound full length of shank.
Hook: As in previous Palmers.

PURPLE PALMER

Body: Purple floss silk, ribbed silver wire.
Hackle: As in Black Palmer.
Hook: No. 14 or 16.
  (All the Palmer flies make good wet flies if dressed with hen hackle.)

IRON BLUE DUN

Tail: Three fibres from iron blue hackle.
Body: Three turns of red tying silk next to tail, rest of body slate grey fur.
Hackle: Iron blue.
Hook: No. 14 or 16.

OLIVE DUN

Tail: Three fibres of light olive.
Body: Light olive quill.
Hackle: Olive dun cock.
Hook: No. 14, 16 or 18.

WICKHAM'S FANCY

Tail: Three fibres ginger-red cock hackle.
Body: Flat gold tinsel.
Hackle: Tied in by tip next to tail and wound to the head.
Hook: No. 14 or 16.

RED SPINNER

Tail: Three fibres of red cock hackle.
Body: Red floss silk, ribbed fine gold wire.

Hackle: Red cock.
Hook: No. 14 or 16.

GINGER SPINNER

Tail: Two fibres from ginger cock hackle.
Body: Light cinnamon quill.
Hackle: Ginger cock.
Hook: No. 16.

BLACK GNAT

Body: Black tying silk. ·
Hackle: Rusty black cock.
Hook: No. 16.

OLIVE QUILL

Tail: Three fibres of olive cock.
Body: Olive quill.
Hackle: Olive cock.
Hook: No. 16.

COCH-Y-BONDHU

Body: Bronze peacock herl.
Hackle: Furnace cock.
Hook: No. 14 or 16.

BADGER AND GOLD

Body: Flat gold tinsel, ribbed fine gold wire.
Hackle: Badger cock.
Hook: No. 16.

ROUGH OLIVE

Tail: Three fibres, olive cock.
Body: Olive seal's wool, ribbed fine gold wire.
Hackle: Olive cock.
Hook: No. 16.

RED TAG

Tail: Red ibis or red wool one-eighth of an inch long.
Body: Bronze peacock herl.
Hackle: Red cock.
Hook: No. 14 or 16.

BLACK SPIDER

> *Body:* Black ostrich herl or seal's wool, ribbed fine silver wire.
> *Hackle:* Black cock.
> *Hook:* No. 16.

RED SPIDER

> *Body:* Red ostrich herl or seal's wool, ribbed fine gold wire.
> *Hackle:* Red cock.
> *Hook:* No. 16 or 18.

MAYFLY (GREEN DRAKE)

> *Tail:* Three fibres (one inch long) cock pheasant tail.
> *Body:* Light olive floss silk, ribbed fine gold wire.
> *Hackle:* Yellowish green cock with one turn of light olive French partridge breast feather.
> *Hook:* No. 10 or 12 long shank.

Dry Flies (Winged)

In practically all dry (winged) flies the cocked wings are created from sections of feathers taken from right and left wings.

MARCH BROWN

> *Tail:* Three fibres of bronze mallard feather.
> *Body:* Light and dark hare's fur, well mixed, ribbed gold tying silk or fine gold wire.
> *Hackle:* Dark mottled partridge.
> *Wings:* Cock pheasant feathers from near shoulder which are nicely mottled.
> *Hook:* No. 12, 14 or 16.

GREENWELL'S GLORY

> *Body:* Yellow waxed tying silk, ribbed fine gold wire.
> *Hackle:* Furnace cock.
> *Wings:* Hen blackbird, sections to be taken from near tip of feathers.
> *Hook:* No. 14 or 16.

WICKHAM'S FANCY

Tail: Three fibres of ginger cock.
Body: Flat gold tinsel.
Hackle: Tied in by tip next to tail and wound to the head.
Wings: Starling wing feathers.
Hook: No. 12, 14 or 16.

IRON BLUE DUN

Tail: Three fibres from iron blue hackle.
Body: Three turns of red tying silk next to tail, rest of body slate-grey fur.
Hackle: Iron blue.
Wings: From starling feathers.
Hook: No. 14 or 16.

RED SPINNER

Tail: Three fibres red cock hackle.
Body: Red floss silk, ribbed fine gold wire.
Hackle: Red cock.
Wings: Light starling wing feathers.
Hook: No. 14 or 16.

OLIVE DUN

Tail: Three fibres light olive cock.
Body: Light olive quill.
Hackle: Olive dun cock.
Wings: From starling feathers.
Hook: No. 14 or 16.

GRANNOM

Body: One turn of green floss silk at end of hook shank, remainder dark heron herl.
Hackle: Ginger cock.
Wings: Partridge wings.
Hook: No. 14 or 16.

BLUE DUN

Tail: Three fibres dark olive cock.
Body: Waxed olive tying silk, ribbed fine gold wire.

Hackle: Dark olive cock.
Wings: Starling.
Hook: No. 14 or 16.

PALE WATERY DUN

Tail: Three fibres pale olive cock.
Body: Very pale yellow quill.
Hackle: Pale olive.
Wings: Light starling feathers.
Hook: No. 14 or 16.

FIERY BROWN

Body: Fiery-brown seal's wool.
Hackle: Red cock.
Wings: Woodcock wing feathers.
Hook: No. 14 or 16.

ALDER

Body: Bronze peacock herl.
Hackle: Black cock.
Wings: From hen pheasant's mottled tail feathers.
Hook: No. 14.

WHITE MOTH

Body: White floss silk, ribbed with yellow tying silk.
Hackle: White cock.
Wings: White duck feathers.
Hook: No. 12 or 14.

BROWN MOTH

Body: Dark hare's fur.
Hackle: Reddish-brown cock.
Wings: Brown duck.
Hook: No. 10, 12 or 14.

YELLOW MOTH

Body: Dark yellow floss silk, ribbed fine gold wire.
Hackle: Ginger cock.
Wings: White duck dyed dark yellow.

Hook: No. 12 or 14.

(The three moths previously described are used when late evening or night fishing.)

BEE FLY

Tail: Consists of small tag of one turn of orange floss silk, rest of body black seal's wool, ribbed with fine gold wire.
Hackle: Black cock.
Wings: From jay wing feathers.
Hook: No. 14 or 16.

WASP FLY

Body: Gold seal's wool, ribbed fine gold wire and bronze peacock herl.
Hackle: Furnace cock.
Wings: Same as bee fly.
Hook: No. 14 or 16.

LIGHT SEDGE

Body: Reddish-brown hare's fur.
Hackle: Pale-red cock.
Wings: Landrail's wing feathers.
Hook: No. 14 or 16.

DARK SEDGE

Body: Brown and black seal's wool mixed.
Hackle: Dark-red cock.
Wings: As in light sedge.
Hook: No. 14 or 16.

COACHMAN

Body: Bronze peacock herl.
Hackle: Can be brown or black cock.
Wings: White duck.
Hook: No. 12, 14 or 16.

Nymph Dressings

MARCH BROWN

Tail: Three one-eighth of an inch fibres of brown partridge feather.
Wing cases: Section of woodcock mottled wing.
Body: Brown hare's fur or seal's wool, ribbed fine gold wire.
Hackle: Dark partridge, one turn and then cut to about one-sixth of an inch.
Hook: No. 14 or 16.

IRON BLUE

Tail: Three one-eighth of an inch fibres from grey cock hackle.
Wing cases: Jay wing feather section and rolled.
Body: Slaty-grey fur or seal's wool.
Thorax: Same as body.
Hackle: One turn iron blue, cut short.
Hook: No. 16.

GRANNOM

Tail: Three short fibres black cock hackle.
Wing cases: Section from starling wing feather and rolled.
Body: Dark hare's fur.
Hackle: Black cock, one turn with fibres cut short.
Hook: No. 16.

BLUE DUN

Tail: Three short fibres dark olive hackle.
Wing cases: Starling or jay feather section, rolled.
Body: Dark olive and blue-grey seal's wool mixed and ribbed fine gold wire.
Hackle: One turn dark olive hackle, cut short.
Hook: No. 16.

OLIVE DUN

Body: Light olive seal's wool, ribbed fine gold wire.
Wing cases: Light starling, tied in midway on shank.
Hackle: One turn light olive hackle.
Hook: No. 16.

Grayling Fly Dressings

I have caught grayling on quite a number of trout-flies, including Greenwell's Glory, Wickham's Fancy, Red Tag, Red Spinner and Iron Blue Dun. However, there are one or two other flies created solely for the grayling angler. They can be dressed for wet or dry-fly fishing.

THE WITCH

Tail: Red ibis or red wool tag.
Body: Green and bronze peacock herl mixed.
Hackle: Badger or grey-dun cock.
Hook: No. 14 or 16.

GOLD WITCH

Tail: Red ibis or red wool tag.
Body: Flat gold tinsel, ribbed fine gold wire.
Hackle: Red cock.
Wings: Light starling.
Hook: No. 14 or 16.

SILVER WITCH

Tail: Red ibis or red wool tag.
Body: Green peacock herl from peacock sword feather, ribbed silver wire.
Hackle: Badger cock.
Hook: No. 14 or 16.

ORANGE TAG

This excellent fly has the same dressing as Red Tag with the exception of the tail which is an orange tag.

APPLE GREEN

Tail: Is formed of a green tag of wool.
Body: Green floss silk, ribbed gold wire.
Hackle: Furnace cock.
Hook: No. 14 or 16.

BRADSHAW'S FANCY

Tail: Red wool tag.
Body: Green and grey seal's wool mixed, ribbed gold wire.

Hackle: Badger cock.
Head: Extending slightly over the eye of the hook is a second red tag. This is also of red wool.
Hook: No. 14 or 16.

LITTLE CHAP

Body: Green and bronze peacock herl mixed.
Hackle: Dun cock.
(This fly can also be dressed with a red tag.)
Hook: No. 14 or 16.

THE GRASSHOPPER

The name of this artificial is a misnomer, in that it is not a fly at all, but is more of a grub in appearance. Dressing is as follows:

Body: Grey seal's wool, tapered to look like a grub fairly fat in the middle. The whole is covered with green and bronze peacock herl, three fibres are used and these are wound on together. The head is given a couple of turns of green peacock herl.
Hook: No. 10 or 12.

This artificial is fished sink and draw. Some grayling anglers I have spoken to say the putting on of a couple of maggots adds to its luring qualities.

13

SEA-TROUT FLIES AND DRESSINGS

In the main, flies to lure this gamester from the sea are more colourful than those used for trout. It is also a fairly recognized fact that by and large the best catches are made during late evening and after dark.

Quite a number of dressings already described for trout are also used for sea-trout. For instance flies with teal, mallard, woodcock and grouse wings all have their devotees among anglers. However, there is one fly which practically every angler seems to use on his cast, it is the Mallard and Claret. For my part, whenever I am fishing for this near relative of the salmon it is always on my cast of flies.

The dressing has already been given in the previous chapter, but the illustrations will show how easily it is to make.

In drawing No. 1 the tail of four tippet fibres has been put in and in No. 2 a short length of gold wire is put on. No. 3 sees the claret dyed seal's wool spun on to the tying thread and No. 4 shows the completed body. In No. 5 we have the hackle in position and No. 6 reveals what the finished fly should look like. The hook can be No. 10 or 12.

Dressings of some other sea-trout flies follow:

BLACK AND GREEN

 Tail: Red wool tag.
 Body: Green seal's wool, ribbed gold oval tinsel.
 Hackle: Black.
 Wings: Black jay feather, rolled.
 Hook: No. 8, 10 or 12.

ORANGE JAY

 Tail: Four fibres cock pheasant tail.

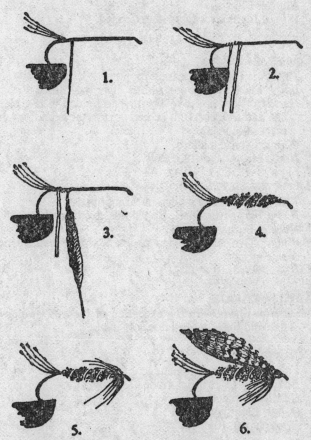

Dressing Mallard and Claret Sea-Trout Fly

1. Tail is put on
2. Gold wire tied in
3. Claret seal's wool spun on
   tying silk
4. Body is complete
5. Hackle tied in
6. Completed fly

c

Body: Orange seal's wool, ribbed gold oval tinsel.
Hackle: Blue jay.
Wings: Light jay wing feathers, rolled.
Hook: No. 10 or 12.

CONNEMARA BLACK

Tail: Small golden pheasant topping.
Body: Black seal's wool, ribbed silver oval tinsel.
Hackle: There are two. The first to be tied in is a black hen and the second to be tied next to the head is a well-marked blue jay.
Wings: Bronze mallard.
Hook: No. 8, 10 or 12.

TIPPET AND SILVER

Tail: Four fibres of golden pheasant tippet.
Body: Flat silver tinsel, ribbed final oval tinsel.
Hackle: Furnace.
Wings: Two small golden pheasant tippet feathers tied side by side.
Hook: No. 8, 10 or 12.

TIPPET AND GOLD

Same as above with the exception of the body which is flat gold tinsel, ribbed fine gold oval.

BLAE AND SILVER

Tail: Four fibres of tippet.
Body: Flat silver tinsel, ribbed final oval tinsel.
Hackle: Furnace.
Wings: Light jay, rolled.
Hook: No. 8, 10 or 12.

14

LURES, DEMONS, TERRORS AND STREAMERS

IN my salmon and sea-trout fly-box are a number of long-eared creations which go by unusual names. In this country we have lures, demons and terrors and in the U.S.A., Canada and New Zealand there is the streamer.

It was in Devon on the River Tavy more than fifty years ago that I first saw a lure in operation. The angler using it was night fishing for sea-trout. In three hours he caught seven nice sea-trout and an eight-pound salmon. Since that day lures have been included in my flies for sea-trout whenever I have gone night fishing.

Making a Tavy (Alexandra lure) is simplicity itself. In the accompanying sketch No. 1 shows a one-and-a-half-inch length of 10 lb. nylon in which two simple knots have been tied.

Drawing No. 2 shows the length of nylon tied to the hooks, which are in line, tandem fashion. The reason for the knots is that it prevents the hook pulling out. One might ask why not fasten it to the eye of the hook. Reason for not doing so is that the hook would flop and would not remain on an even keel when being used.

Drawing No. 3, the tails, silver bodies and hackles have been put on. The tails are composed of fibres of red ibis and the hackles are blue jay.

Drawing No. 4 illustrates the finished fly. The wings are composed of fourteen lengths of green and bronze peacock herl, which over-lap a strip of red ibis. A small jungle cock feather is placed on each side. I have found that if the herl is moistened between thumb and forefinger it is much more tractable and will lie nicely along the back of the tandem.

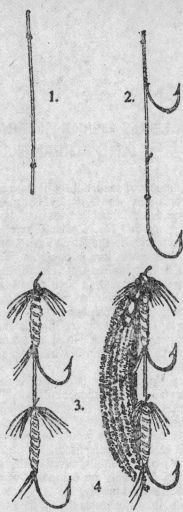

Making a Tavy (Alexandra Lure)
1. Length of 10 lb. nylon with simple knots
2. Hooks are fixed tandem fashion
3. Silver body and black hackles
4. Completed lure with peacock herl wings

There are many types and patterns of lures but the general principle of dressing them is about the same.

The TERROR has three hooks (see sketch) but here again the method of dressing is the same.

The DEMON is constructed of two hooks, but in some patterns the tail hook is a double one. Silver Blue and Dunkeld are two that invariably have a double hook instead of the usual single. In my experience a lure, demon or terror that has a double hook attached does not work so well in the water, furthermore it is my considered opinion that it

A Three-Hooked Terror

does not hold so well when a fish is hooked, one hook acting as a lever against the other.

We now come to STREAMERS and in general appearance it is not unlike our lure or terror, but it differs in that it is dressed on a long-shanked hook. The rigid foundation of the American creation enables it to work on an even keel, as against a decided tail wobble of the lure or terror.

There are dozens of patterns, but each and every one has been created to represent either a minnow or an immature fish and as we all know trout in particular when they get any size relish minnows and other small fish as their main course with flies as dessert.

In Canada and the U.S.A. hundreds of salmon and steel-head trout (migratory rainbow trout) are caught every year on streamer flies. Today the streamer is beginning to play a major part as a 'killer' among the salmon, trout and sea-trout in the British Isles.

The Black Ghost is a favourite of mine and for that

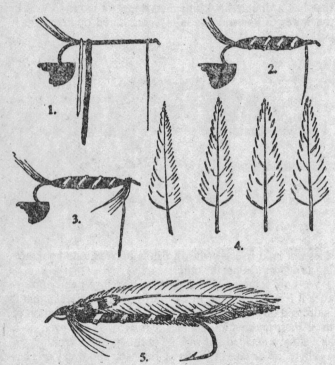

Making a Black Ghost Streamer Fly

1. Long-shanked hook in vice, tail, tinsel and black floss silk is tied in
2. The completed body
3. Hackle is added
4. Four hackle feathers for wings
5. The finished Streamer Fly

reason has been selected as the subject for the drawings and description of how to dress it. Nearly all streamers follow the same ideas in dressing, in that cock hackles are used in the making of the wings.

In the first sketch a small golden pheasant topping feather has been tied in for the tail and a length of oval silver tinsel (medium size) and a length of black floss silk.

The second drawing illustrates how the body should look when the surplus floss and tinsel has been trimmed off.

In the third sketch a hackle composed of fibres from a golden pheasant topping feather has been put on.

The fifth and final sketch illustrates what the finished fly should look like. The varnish at the head is black. Occasionally I have seen a Black Ghost with a head made of black ostrich herl, but in my opinion this final adornment is not necessary. The wings of the Black Ghost are white and are from the neck hackles of a White Leghorn cock.

Here are the dressings of some other good lures, terrors and streamers. We will deal with lures first:

SILVER BLUE LURE

Body: The shanks of both hooks are flat silver tinsel, ribbed final oval silver tinsel.
Hackle: Furnace.
Wings: Two strips of teal or well-marked grey mallard.
Hooks: No. 10 in tandem.

PETER ROSS

Tail: Six fibres of tippet.
Body: Shank of first hook is flat silver tinsel, ribbed oval silver tinsel. Second shank is red seal's wool, ribbed fine silver wire.
Hackle: Furnace or black.
Wings: Two strips of well-marked teal.
Hooks: No. 10 in tandem.

CINNAMON AND SILVER

Body: The shanks of both hooks are flat silver tinsel, ribbed final oval silver tinsel.

Hackle: Furnace or black.
Wings: Cinnamon turkey or hen wing feather, rolled.
Hooks: No. 10 or 12.

Terrors

BLUE TERROR

Tails: The end hook and middle hook have tails of red wool.
Body: Flat silver tinsel, ribbed oval silver on all three hooks.
Hackle: Blue.
Wings: Two blue hackle feathers and over them bronze mallard.
Hooks: No. 12.

CRESTED MALLARD

Body: All three hooks are flat silver, ribbed oval silver. (There is no hackle.)
Wings: Two strips of bronze mallard with a golden pheasant topping over and reaching just beyond end hook.
Hooks: No. 12.

JUNGLE COCK AND SILVER

Body: All three hooks flat silver tinsel, ribbed oval silver. (No hackle.)
Wings: Two long jungle cock feathers reaching to just beyond the end hook.
Hooks: No. 10 or 12.
(The length of all terrors should not exceed two and a half inches.)

Streamers

GREY GHOST STREAMER

Body: Orange floss silk, ribbed oval silver tinsel.
Hackle: Four bronze peacock herl fibres reaching to just

beyond the end of hook, and four white hackle fibres same length as herl.

Wings: Two blue-grey hackle feathers extending half an inch beyond hook.

Cheeks: Silver pheasant black and white breast feather. Jungle cock on top.

Hook: No. 6 or 8 long-shank.

LADY GHOST

Body: Flat oval tinsel, ribbed oval silver.

Hackle: Four fibres of bronze peacock herl and four fibres of white hackle extending beyond end of hook.

Wings: Two honey-badger hackles to half an inch beyond hook.

Cheeks: Reddish-brown feather from cock pheasant's breast, with small jungle cock feather on top.

Hook: No. 6 or 8 long-shank.

BLUE DEVIL

Tail: Golden pheasant red breast feather.

Body: Flat gold tinsel, ribbed oval gold.

Hackle: Well-marked Plymouth Rock cock with some fibres of golden pheasant topping mixed in.

Wings: Four Plymouth Rock cock hackles, extending half an inch beyond end of hook.

Cheeks: Small blue peacock and kingfisher feathers.

Hook: No. 6 or 8 long-shank.

SPENCER BAY

Tail: Six tippet fibres quarter of an inch long.

Body: Silver tinsel, ribbed oval silver tinsel.

Hackle: Mixed light blue and yellow cock dyed feathers.

Wings: Two honey-badger cock hackles extending half an inch beyond hook.

Cheeks: Reddish-brown feather from cock pheasant's breast, with jungle cock on top.

Hook: No. 6 or 8 long-shank.

WHITE MARABOU

Body: Flat silver tinsel, ribbed oval silver.

Hackle: Scarlet cock.

Wings: White marabou herl, twelve fibres with half a
dozen green peacock fibres on top, extending beyond
end of hook.

Shoulders: Jungle cock.

Hook: No. 6 or 8 long-shank.

15

DRESSING SALMON-FLIES

IN dressing salmon-flies the preparatory work, particularly
with the feathers concerned, takes a little longer, but it is
not complicated or difficult to master.

Quite a number of patterns have 'made-up' wings; by
that I mean that fibres of different feathers and different
colours are placed together to form wings. The operation is
generally known as 'marrying'.

The feathers of a goose, swan, turkey and bustard are
fairly easy to build into one whole, but duck feathers like
teal and summer duck are not so easy.

However, in marrying fibres one important fact must
always be borne in mind. It is this. If you take your first
fibre from a right wing of a bird then the rest of the fibres
must be from the right wings of the required feathers in
making that particular wing. The same principle applies to
left wings.

To get the strips of red, blue and yellow fibres, dyed
goose or swan feathers are used. Take a couple of fibres
from a red feather, the same from a blue and yellow and
place them side by side and press them close together.
Then pick them up, butt first between the thumb and index
finger of your right hand. With the thumb and index finger
of the left hand stroke the fibres upward and the fibres will
stick together as if drawn by a magnet. Reason for this is
that each individual fibre has small curved hairs that inter-
lock with the hairs of the other fibres in much the same way
as a zip fastener on a bag does.

Always take the fibres as long as possible as the butts do
not knit together as well as the ends. You can always cut
them to length after you have completed making the wing.

Quite a number of patterns have a body hackle; this is

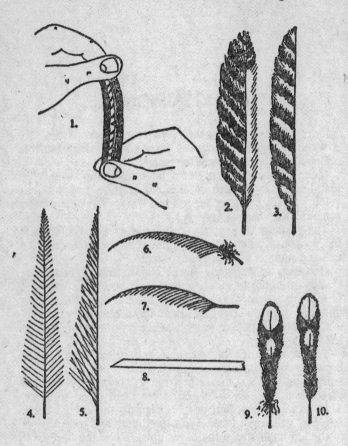

Preparing Salmon-Fly Feathers

1. Marrying different feather fibres
2. Blue Jay feather
3. Jay feather prepared
4. Hackle feather
5. Doubled hackle feather
6. Golden Pheasant topping feather
7. Prepared topping feather
8. Tinsel with wedge end
9. Jungle cock feather
10. Prepared Jungle Cock

just as easy to do as making a mixed wing. It is known as
'doubling' a hackle, the general idea being to have all the
fibres lying on one side of the stem only. The best method
that I know of to accomplish this is to attach a pair of
hackle pliers to each end of the hackle, then hang the
hackle, bright side downwards, over the forefinger of the
right hand. The weight of the pliers will generally tend to
make the two sides of fibres stand up from the finger. A
slight pull on the pliers and the fibres of one side will come
up to a right-angle with those of the other side.

With the thumb of the right hand stroke the fibres from
right to left, at the same time pressing firmly on the fibres.
After a few seconds it will be found that the fibres will stay
over in the desired position.

A hackle so treated has a great advantage over a hackle
used in the ordinary way. It enables it to be wound in front
or behind a body ribbing with ease and without the fibres
getting intermixed or deranged.

The blue jay feather which is such a feature in some fly
hackles needs a little preparation before it is ready for use.
The colourless side of the feather is stripped off and the
stem where it has been taken from has the pith taken away
from it with a razor blade so that it can be wound easily.

Golden pheasant toppings also need a little attention
before they can be used. After the fluff has been stripped
off the fly is crimped at the butt end with a thumb nail. By
doing this the topping can be easily tied in.

Jungle cock feathers also need the fluff stripping off.

To get the flat tinsel to sit nicely it is always best to cut
the end that is to be tied in into the shape of a wedge.

The illustration accompanying this chapter will assist the
amateur in the carrying out of the various little jobs en-
tailed.

Before we get down to the job of making a salmon-fly it
might be a good idea for the beginner to get acquainted
with the names of the various parts that go to make up a fly.

A glance at the drawing, Parts of a salmon-fly, will prove
of considerable assistance in this respect. However, No. 12
on the drawing, HORNS, is not so important these days. In

the past practically every salmon-fly had these adornments but in the main they have been omitted by dressers nowadays and flies seem to attract just as well. Therefore the new-comer can please himself as to whether horns are included or not.

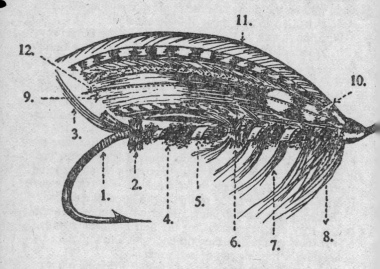

Parts of a Salmon-Fly

1. Tag	7. Body hackle
2. Butt	8. Throat hackle
3. Tail	9. Wing
4. Body	10. Cheek
5. Tinsel ribbing	11. Topping
6. Middle butt	12. Horns (optional)

16

DRESSING A THUNDER AND LIGHTNING
AND A DURHAM RANGER

WE are now ready to dress our first salmon-fly and I can
think of no easier one to start with than a THUNDER
AND LIGHTNING. This particular pattern is a favourite
with most anglers as it can be used throughout the whole
season; indeed, a very close friend of mine relies on three
patterns throughout a season – Jock Scott, Thunder and
Lightning and Durham Ranger; what is more he kills quite
a number of fish every season.

Before starting to dress a salmon-fly it is a good idea to
have the materials ready on the table. We shall need fine
gold wire, yellow floss silk, black ostrich herl, one orange-
coloured cock hackle that has been doubled, black floss
silk, oval gold tinsel, a left and right section of brown mallard (well-marked), two medium-sized jungle cock feathers,
a prepared blue jay feather and a golden pheasant topping
which is put on last of all.

Here then is how to dress a Thunder and Lightning:

In the first sketch a tag of four turns of gold wire and
three turns of gold floss silk has been tied in together with
a small golden pheasant topping which constitutes the tail.

In drawing No. 2 a butt of black ostrich herl is in position, along with the doubled orange body hackle, while the
body of black floss silk ribbed with oval gold tinsel is made.
In the next sketch the body hackle has been wound to near
the head, each turn of the hackle being behind the gold
ribbing and the throat hackle of blue jay is tied in. In the
next drawing two sections of brown mallard one from a left
wing feather and the other from a right feather has been
put on and the jungle cock feathers are placed at the side.

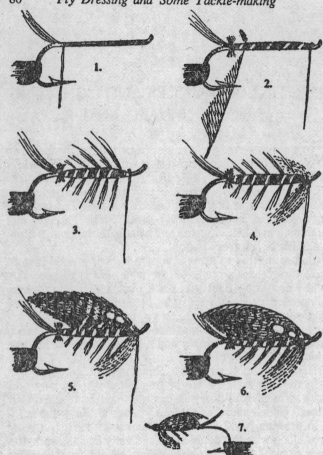

Thunder and Lightning

1. Tag and tail put in
2. The body is made and doubled hackle ready for ribbing
3. The hackle is wound on
4. Jay hackle is put on
5. Brown Mallard and Jungle Cock in position
6. Completed fly with Golden Pheasant topping tied in.
7. Low-water fly

All we have to do now is put on the golden-pheasant topping, which must sit nice and close to the back of the mallard, taper off the head with the whip-finish, which is then given a coat of black varnish and the fly is complete as seen in drawing No. 6.

I usually dress my Thunder and Lightnings on No. 6 for general season fishing and No. 2 for early season work. The former is about an inch in length and the latter about an inch and a quarter which does not include the up-turned eye. Of course if one is going to fish a full and very big river it might be a good idea to make a couple on No. 1 irons, such hooks are about one and a half inches in length.

For low-water fly fishing the hook is forged out of a little finer wire and the dressing usually starts half-way on the shank and is much smaller. By experience I have found that Nos. 6, 7 and 8 low-water hooks are best.

Durham Ranger

For this fly we shall require the following materials: Silver wire, yellow floss silk, one small and one large topping, flat silver tinsel and fine oval silver tinsel, a small Indian crow (red) feather, dark orange and black seal's wool, one double badger hackle dyed orange and a light blue hackle, four tippet feathers, two large and two small, four jungle cock feathers, two large and two small, a blue chatterer or kingfisher and the black varnish.

Like the Thunder and Lightning, the Durham Ranger is a good all-round season fly in all parts of the British Isles and what is more is just as easy to dress. On large-size hooks it is a very good early-season fly and for mid-season and low water, flies dressed on Nos. 8, 9 and 10 hooks take quite a few good fish every year.

Here then is how to make a Durham Ranger:

In the first drawing we have the tag of silver wire and yellow floss silk, four turns each, together with the tail, comprised of a golden pheasant topping and small Indian crow in position and the butt of black ostrich herl is on also.

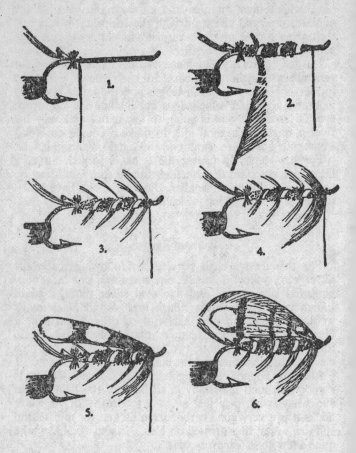

Durham Ranger

1. Tag, tail and butt in position
2. Body and body hackle
3. Body hackle in place
4. Throat hackle complete
5. Jungle Cock tied in
6. Completed fly

The second sketch illustrates how the three-part body orange, fiery brown and black seal's wool, ribbed flat silver tinsel should look before the body hackle is tied in. In No. 3 the body hackle is in place and No. 4 has the throat hackle of light blue complete. The long jungle cock feathers are tied in, bright side outwards. The last drawing shows the four tippets in position, jungle cock sides and topping over all.

17

FAMOUS SALMON-FLIES AND DRESSINGS

IT is estimated that there are about 350 different salmon-fly patterns in this country, but the twenty described in this chapter are among the more famous. We start off with:

JOCK SCOTT

Tag: Silver wire and yellow floss silk.
Tail: Golden pheasant topping and Indian crow.
Butt: Black ostrich herl.
Body: In two equal parts. The half near the tail is yellow floss silk, ribbed oval silver tinsel. A black ostrich herl butt is put on and then a couple of orange feathers either side of the butt. The second half is black floss silk ribbed oval silver. A black hackle is put in and over it a natural guinea-fowl hackle is tied in for the throat.
Wings: Two strips of dark mottled and white-tipped turkey tail and the remainder (both wings) are built up of blue, yellow and red swan, golden pheasant tail, bustard, green peacock wing, brown mallard and grey mallard. Topping.
Sides: Jungle cock.
Cheeks: Blue chatterer or kingfisher.
Head: Black varnish.

BLACK RANGER

With the exception of the body, which is black floss silk, the dressing is the same as the Durham Ranger.

RED RANGER

This fly has a red floss silk body, but in every other way. is the same as the other two rangers.

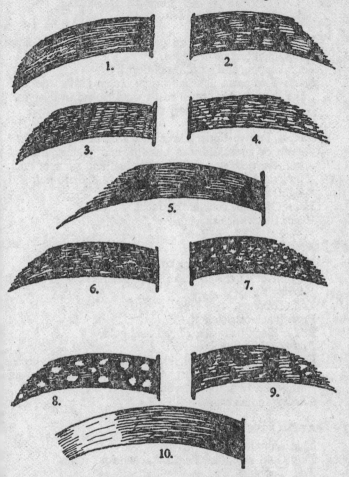

Some Natural Feathers

1. Cinnamon Turkey Tail	6. Light Brown Mottled Turkey
2. Golden Pheasant Tail	7. Dark Brown Mottled Turkey
3. Brown Mallard	8. Guinea-Fowl Tail
4. Grey Mottled Turkey	9. Speckled Turkey
5. Florican Bustard	10. Turkey White Tip Tail

FIERY BROWN

Tag: Four turns gold wire and the same number of floss silk, light orange in colour.

Tail: Topping and six fibres of tippet.

Body: Two parts, first half bright orange seal's wool and the second fiery-brown seal's wool ribbed oval silver.

Body hackle: Doubled fiery-brown.

Throat hackle: Blue jay.

Wings: Twelve tippet fibres, fibres of blue, red, yellow swan or goose, florican bustard, and golden pheasant tail (married) and fine strips of teal and summer duck (married) with two sections of brown mallard (left and right) on top with topping over all.

Sides: Of jungle cock are optional.

Head: Black varnish.

BLACK GOLDFINCH

This is an excellent fly for Irish waters.

Tag: Silver wire, four turns and the same number of gold floss silk.

Tail: Topping.

Butt: Black ostrich herl.

Body: Black floss silk, ribbed oval gold.

Body hackle: Blue jay.

Wings: Twelve fibres of tippet partly covered by broad sections (left and right) and deep yellow and red swan or goose. Four toppings on top.

Cheeks: Indian crow.

GOLDEN OLIVE

This is another good Irish fly.

Tag: Gold wire, blue floss silk, each four turns.

Tail: Topping.

Butt: Black ostrich herl.

Body: Golden yellow floss silk or seal's wool, ribbed oval gold.

Body hackle: Doubled golden olive.

Throat hackle: Blue jay.

Wings: Twelve tippet fibres and fibres of blue, yellow, orange and green swan or goose, bustard, golden pheasant tail (married) and narrow strips of teal and summer duck (married). Left and right sections of brown mallard on top and topping over all.

Head: Black varnish.

BLUE CHARM

Tag: Silver wire and yellow floss silk, four turns each.

Tail: Topping.

Butt: Black ostrich herl.

Body: Black floss silk, ribbed oval silver tinsel.

Throat hackle: Dark blue.

Wings: Dark brown speckled turkey tail feather and a narrow strip of teal on top with a topping over all.

Head: Black varnish.

DUSTY MILLER

Tag: Silver wire and yellow floss silk, four turns each.

Tail: Topping and Indian crow.

Butt: Black ostrich herl.

Body: Embossed flat silver tinsel, ribbed fine oval silver tinsel for two-thirds of the shank, followed by orange floss silk oval silver.

Throat hackle: Natural guinea-fowl.

Wings: Married strips of brown mottled turkey tail, golden pheasant tail, bustard and guinea-fowl with a strip of brown mallard over and topping over all.

Sides: Small jungle cock.

Head: Black varnish.

BLUE DOCTOR

Tag: Silver wire and yellow floss silk four turns each.

Tail: Topping and blue kingfisher.

Butt: Scarlet ostrich herl or wool.

Body: Light blue floss silk, ribbed silver oval tinsel.

Body hackle: Light blue.

Throat hackle: Blue jay.

Wings: Tippet fibres, guinea-fowl, golden pheasant tail, light mottled turkey tail, teal, yellow and light blue swan, red ibis and brown mallard on top, topping to finish.

Cheeks: Blue kingfisher.

Head: Red varnish.

BLACK DOSE

Tag: Orange floss silk.

Tail: Topping, teal and ibis.

Body: One-third light blue seal's wool, remainder black seal's wool. Ribbing is made by teasing out the black wool with hat-pin or dubbing needle.

Throat hackle: Light claret.

Wings: Two tippets side by side, teal, mottled turkey tail, golden pheasant tail, summer duck, peacock herl, ibis and brown mallard.

Head: Black varnish.

LEMON GREY

Tag: Silver wire and yellow floss silk.

Tail: Topping.

Butt: Black ostrich.

Body: Silver-grey seal's wool, ribbed oval silver.

Throat hackle: Blue.

Wings: Two broad sections of brown mallard (left and right), two narrow sections of teal on top with topping over.

Head: Black varnish.

DUNKELD

Tag: Gold wire and orange floss silk.

Tail: Topping and two small jungle cock one either side of topping.

Butt: Black ostrich herl.

Body: Flat gold tinsel, ribbed oval gold.

Body hackle: Orange.

Throat hackle: Blue jay.

Wings: Two strips peacock wing, brown mallard, blue, red and yellow swan and topping.

Cheeks: Blue kingfisher.

Head: Black varnish.

JEANNIE

Tag: Silver wire.
Tail: Topping.
Body: One-third yellow floss silk, remainder black floss silk, ribbed oval silver.
Throat hackle: Black.
Wings: Brown mallard, topping over.
Sides: Jungle cock.
Head: Black varnish.

GREEN HIGHLANDER

Tag: Silver wire, pale yellow floss silk.
Tail: Topping and teal.
Butt: Black ostrich herl.
Body: One-third yellow floss silk, remainder pale green seal's wool, ribbed oval silver.
Body hackle: Pale green.
Wings: Two tippets, light bustard, golden pheasant tail, dark mottled turkey, fibres of yellow and green swan, brown mallard, topping over all.
Sides: Jungle cock (optional).
Head: Black.

JOCKIE

Tag: Silver wire.
Tail: Topping.
Body: One-third yellow floss silk, remainder black floss silk, ribbed oval silver.
Throat hackle: Furnace.
Wings: Brown mallard.
Sides: Jungle cock.
Head: Black varnish.

SILVER WILKINSON

Tag: Silver wire.
Tail: Topping and small tippet.
Butt: Scarlet ostrich herl or wool.
Body: Flat silver ribbed oval silver.
Throat hackle: Blue and magenta-coloured hackles.

Wings: Tippet fibres, golden pheasant tail over-married
   wings of red, blue and yellow swan, bustard, brown
   mottled turkey tail, strips of teal and summer duck.
   Topping on top.
Cheeks: Blue kingfisher.
Sides: Jungle cock (optional).

MAR LODGE

Tag: Silver wire.
Tail: Topping and jungle cock.
Butt: Black ostrich herl.
Body: In three parts. Nos. 1 and 3 of silver flat tinsel,
   No. 2 of black floss silk, all the body ribbed oval silver.
Throat hackle: Natural guinea-fowl.
Wings: Fibres of red, blue and yellow swan (married)
   and strips of peacock wing, grey mallard, dark mottled
   turkey wing or tail, golden pheasant tail, topping on
   top.
Sides: Jungle cock (not too large).
Head: Black varnish.

BROWN TURKEY

Tag: Gold wire.
Tail: Topping, teal and red ibis.
Body: Half orange and half black seal's wool, ribbed
   oval gold.
Hackle: Black.
Wings: Light brown mottled turkey tail, topping over.
Sides: Jungle cock.
Head: Black varnish.

ROGUE

Tag: Gold wire.
Tail: Orange and yellow swan.
Body: Two parts, orange and black seal's wool, ribbed
   oval silver.
Wings: Yellow, red and blue swan, sections of teal over
   and topping over all.
Sides: Jungle cock (optional).
Head: Black varnish.

AKROYD

Tag: Gold wire.

Tail: Topping and tippet fibres.

Body: First half yellow seal's wool, followed by black seal's wool, ribbed gold oval tinsel.

Body hackle: Black on second half.

Throat hackle: Black heron extending to end of hook.

Wings: Two sections (left and right) of cinnamon turkey tail.

Sides: Jungle cock, tied so that they run at side of heron hackle.

Head: Black varnish.

Shrimps and Lures

In mid-season quite a number of salmon have been caught on artificial shrimps and lures; the two best shrimps I know were brought out by Mr. P. Curry.

RED SHRIMP

Tag: Silver wire or narrow flat silver.

Tail: Red golden pheasant breast feather, wound hackle fashion.

Body: In two parts, first red floss silk, ribbed fine oval silver, second half black floss ribbed a size larger oval silver.

Middle hackle: Well-marked badger.

Head hackle: Badger.

Wings: Two jungle cock feathers, bright side facing each other and extending to end of body.

Head: Red varnish.

GOLDEN SHRIMP

Tag: Silver wire or narrow flat silver.

Tail: Yellow golden pheasant rump feather tied in as hackle.

Body: Two parts, first flat embossed silver, ribbed oval silver, then four small toucan feathers acting as veil followed as first part of body.

Wings: Two jungle cock feathers as in Red Shrimp.

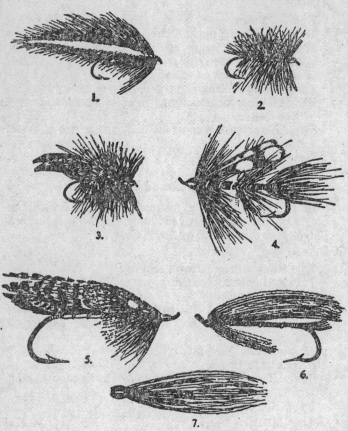

Shrimp and other Flies

1. Blue Elver Lure
2. Badger Palmer
3. Large Sedge
4. Shrimp Fly
5. Silver Sprat
6. Hair Fly
7. Hair tube Fly

Middle hackle: Badger.
Head hackle: Orange or gold.
Head: Red varnish.

Another type of shrimp which I saw lure a couple of
small salmon from the River Teify (Wales) was invented
by Mr. John Bachelor of Croxley Green, Hertfordshire. He
called it Bachelor's Pride. The only difference to a Curry
shrimp was that the head hackle was formed of a long-
fibred peacock blue breast feather. The fibres extending to
beyond the end of the hook. I have taken fish with it on the
River Wye, River Tavy, and the River Balgy, Scotland.

Yet another type of salmon shrimp is dressed like a trout
nymph. The body is pink seal's wool, ribbed oval gold and
a broad section of a pink (dyed) light mottled turkey tail is
tied in at the bend of the hook and brought over to the
head. The wool body is teased out to form a semblance of
legs.

In regard to salmon lures most of the long-shanked
streamer flies already described for sea-trout will lure salmon on occasions.

One type of lure, however, with which my friends and I
have had a fair measure of luck is that known as the Blue
Elver. I first saw it on sale in a Durham County tackle shop.
Here is the dressing:

BLUE ELVER

Tail: Red ibis.
Body: Black floss silk ribbed oval silver.
Hackle: Blue.
Wings: Two Vulturine guinea-fowl, well marked with
   white strip back feathers, tied streamer fashion.
Sides: Jungle cock.
Head: Red.
Hook: No. 6, low-water.

Dry Flies

Dry flies for salmon are not so popular as they should be.
Patterns are generally tied Palmer fashion. When fish are

making head and tail rises repeatedly and will not look at normal flies it is a wise man who changes over to a dry fly. Flies that have been particularly successful include the sedge series and also the alders. They should be dressed on No. 6 low-water hooks.

Low Water Flies

Among the low-water fly patterns we have Thunder and Lightning (already described), Jeannie, Logie, Silver Blue, Blue Charm, March Brown, Silver Doctor, Green Peacock and Lady Caroline.

Sprat Flies

In recent years a number of anglers have, during the early part of the season, used with a fair amount of success, flies that are supposed to imitate the gold and silver sprat; a natural bait that has thousands of devotees. Both flies are fairy easy to create. Here is the dressing of the Silver Sprat:

Tag: Silver wire, six turns.
Tail: Bunched teal fibres.
Body: Flat silver tinsel, ribbed large size oval silver.
Wings: Two half-inch broad blue swan strips, left and right feathers, two Plymouth Rock cock hackles.
First head hackle: Brown and grey mallard mixed. Second head hackle is badger.
Sides: Small jungle cock.
Head: Black varnish.
Hook: No. 5/o ordinary forged. In length this hook is two inches long and heavy enough to get the fly well down.

Golden Sprat

Tag: Six turns gold wire.
Tail: Two golden pheasant toppings.
Body: Gold and pale yellow seal's wool mixed, ribbed large oval gold tinsel.
Wings: Two half-inch broad strips of deep yellow swan,

left and right feathers and four large golden pheasant toppings over all.

Head hackle: Two deep-yellow cock hackles wound on together.

Head: Black varnish.

Hook: Same as Silver Sprat.

Hair Flies

An import from America, these flies have not as yet made their mark over here. However, I know from personal experience that such flies can lure Pacific salmon and I have caught a few Atlantic salmon on them in Canada. In making such flies one uses dyed animal hair and nylon fibres instead of feathers. The sketch will give the general idea of what a hair fly looks like.

In Scotland, of course there are a couple of hair patterns that have been in existence for many years; I refer to the Garry Dog and the Hairy Mary.

The original Garry Dog was made with yellow hair from a dog, but the modern version is a composite sort of a fly in that we have a floss silk body instead of hair and the tail is composed of feathers. In the first one made it was hair.

The Hairy Mary is about fifty years old and the original dressing was all hair. Here are the dressings of the two Scottish flies:

GARRY (YELLOW) DOG

Tag: Silver wire.

Tail: Topping and Indian crow.

Butt: Orange or deep yellow wool.

Body: Black floss silk, ribbed flat silver followed by oval silver.

Hackle: Blue cock.

Wings: Red bucktail or polar bear forms the underwing and on top is placed yellow buck tail or polar bear.

Head: Black varnish.

HAIRY MARY

Tag: Silver wire.
Tail: Topping.
Butt: Black ostrich.
Body: Black floss silk, ribbed oval silver.
Hackle: Deep blue cock.
Wings: Brown deer hair with a few orange and red (dyed)
 hairs intermingled.
Head: Black varnish.
The hooks for both of these flies range from No. 4 to
 No. 6.

Tube Flies

Another quite recent introduction is the tube fly. The
foundation is a small diameter plastic tube and on it is
made the fly, the dressing can be of hair or feathers. A tube
fly looks for all the world like the head of a water-colour
paint-brush. However, I have witnessed some remarkable
catches made by them.

In Devon a friend of mine, Colonel Charles Landale, has
caught a large number of sea-trout on a tube fly he created
from the black hair of a retriever dog. A Welsh farmer who
specializes in goats has lured scores of sea-trout and a few
salmon on tube flies made out of goat's hair.

Plastic tubes are easily obtained for the salmon size in
that most of the cheap ball-point pens have plastic tube ink
reservoirs. When empty an ordinary pipe cleaner can be
pushed through to get rid of what ink remains. You then cut
the size of tube you want to work on. Push a piece of wire
or a nail through the tube so that you can get it to hold in
the vice. It must be a tight fit in the tube or else when you
come to put on the dressing it will turn round.

Some dressers put on tinsel, but I find it makes a less
bulky fly if the tube is painted the colour required, red,
black, silver, gold, etc.

With tube flies one uses feather fibres (instead of whole
feathers and feather sections) and bunches of hair.

For sea-trout and trout tube flies a finer diameter plastic

tube can be purchased very cheaply from any surgical-instrument maker, or dealers in fly-dressing equipment.

Here is how to dress a Black and Silver tube fly:

The tube has been painted a silver colour and is fixed in the vice. A short distance from what will be the head of the fly we put on a spot of clear nail varnish, then tie in the waxed thread. The black hair fibres are arranged in four small bunches, the first one is tied in, the tube turned round a little, the second bunch is fixed and so on. By the time the last fibres are in position the fly should look like sketch No. 7. The head is given a whip-finish and a coat of black varnish.

By subtle use of different-coloured fibres, hair or feather, the fly-dresser can imitate quite a number of salmon-flies.

Last season my family and I caught a large number of mackerel when using three-inch-long tube flies, the dressings of which were multi-coloured nylon fibres. The tubes having been painted silver and blue and black and gold.

I believe there is a great future for tube flies as game-fish producers, but one vital factor should be borne in mind: the treble hook used in conjunction with this type of fly should be the smallest possible, bearing in mind, of course, the type of fish one is hoping to catch.

18

SALT-WATER FLIES

In the last ten years there has been a considerable growth in salt-water fly fishing. Of course flies to lure mackerel, pollack and bass are nothing new, for I remember using a 'Cuddy' fly at Craster (Northumberland) more than fifty years ago. However, in those days sea flies were roughly dressed in comparison to some of the creations one can get these days.

Granted four coloured, red, yellow, blue and white cock hackle feathers tied to a silvered (tinned) long-shanked hook is still the vogue among many coastal anglers to this day. Simple in construction, they still catch their quota of fish every season. This short chapter deals with the more 'polished' type of sea fly.

Flies for salt water that have silver or gold tinsel in their make-up are of little use after a few days for the tinsel loses its brilliance and as a result its luring capabilities fade also. The invention of LUREX has overcome this difficulty and it can be had in gold, silver, red, blue and green and also mixed colours.

Here then are a few dressings for sea flies. In each case the hook is long-shanked, mackerel size.

Silver and Blue

Tail: Red swan or wool.
Body: Silver lurex, ribbed blue lurex.
Hackle: Two blue and white cock hackles wound together.
Wings: Two Plymouth Rock cock hackles dyed blue and two white cock hackles. The four feathers extending to an inch beyond the hook. The two white hackles are tied in first.
Head: Red varnish.

GOLD AND RED

Tail: Red swan or wool.
Body: Gold lurex, ribbed red lurex.
Hackle: Two red cock hackles.
Wings: Two red hackles tied in first and the yellow pair
  on top.
Head: Black varnish.

BLACK AND SILVER

Tail: Red swan or wool.
Body: Silver lurex, ribbed black (doubled) hackle.
Wings: Four black hackles.
Head: Black varnish.

WHITE WINGS

Tail: Red swan or wool.
Body: Silver lurex.
Hackle: Two black cock hackles.
Wings: Four white hackles.
Sides: Jungle cock.
Head: Black varnish.

MIXED WING

Tail: Red swan, or wool.
Body: Silver lurex, ribbed blue lurex.
Hackle: Yellow.
Wings: One red, blue, yellow and white hackles.
Head: Red varnish.

BLUE WINGS

Tail: Red swan or wool.
Body: Silver lurex, ribbed black (doubled) hackle.
Wings: Four deep-blue cock hackles.
Sides: Jungle cock.
Head: Black varnish.

19

FINS, SWIVELS AND OTTERS

A LOT of fishermen start out with the idea that if you're using a spinning bait, natural or artificial, the simple expedient of placing a swivel just ahead of it will automatically remove any danger of a twisted line. I wish it were as simple as that, but the truth is that when the bait spins rapidly, the tendency for the line to twist is too strong for a single swivel, even the ball-bearing type, or even several of them to off-set. Although the swivel revolves easily when there is no pressure on it, the moment there is a pull on each end of the swivel it turns with a certain amount of friction and the tendency to twist the line remains.

And so, something else is required to keep the line kink-free. A keel sinker, one that clamps on to the line and hangs like a weighted fin, will keep the line from twisting if the swivel is placed between it and the spinning bait.

Keel weights are usually heart-shaped and channelled out to make them bend over easily and clamp securely on the line. If you can get hold of some sheet lead from a plumber you can make a couple of dozen, different sizes, in an evening when the water is all against fishing.

Of course any weight that has its centre of gravity well below its fastening point to the line will work well in conjunction with a swivel, but spherical weights and others of near similar design offer more resistance to movement through the water. The keel sinker is especially designed to overcome this problem and it does it beautifully with even

---

Making Keel Sinkers   *Illustration Key*

1. Keel sinker with channel
2. Keel sinker on trace
3. Aluminium anti-kink on trace
4. Line end prepared for splicing
5. The loop is made
6. Completed splice

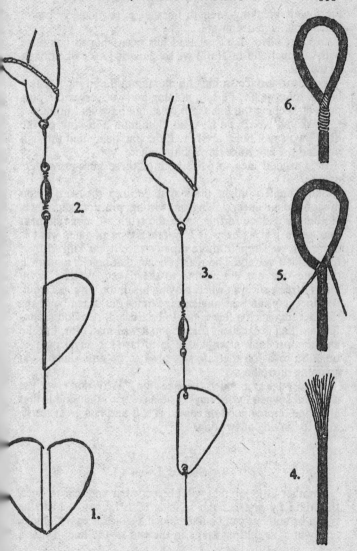

2.

3.

6.

5.

4.

1.

the lowest breaking-strength lines. It is particularly useful when trolling in deep water.

In sketch No. 1 a keel lead has been shaped complete with channel and in No. 2 we see how it looks when fixed to the line.

For near-surface trolling an aluminum fin an inch or two inches long weighs next to nothing and yet serves the purpose of keeping the line from twisting above that point.

In sketch No. 3 we have an aluminum anti-kink on the line. Two small holes are bored, the line being tied through one and the bait trace through the other.

It is a good idea to paint both of these kink-preventers green.

Some anglers might think that because they use nylon monofilament lines kinking or twisting will not take place. Nothing could be farther from the truth. A monofilament line kinks just as easy as any other type of line; what is more it loses strength more rapidly once it has kinked than the braided variety. The reason being that cracks appear in the line that are not visible to the naked eye and when under stress, such as when playing a salmon or good trout, the line snaps and the angler, nine times out of ten bemoans the fact that such a line is not to be trusted. A nylon monofilament line is excellent for the job it was made for, but the angler must look after it if it is to last for any length of time. So to be on the safe side always use anti-kinks when spinning or trolling.

Some anglers ponder the question, 'Why don't we use anti-kinks when fly fishing?' The answer to that one is that a fly line impregnated or coated is stiff and has great resistance to kinking or twisting.

A Spliced Loop

Another little job that will prevent wear and tear to lines, this time fly lines, is the splicing of a loop to which the nylon or gut cast can be fixed. Such a splice is easy to make and will save putting knots in the end of the line. Tying a

line to a cast scrapes off the coating sheath and weakens
the line at this point, allowing damp to creep through the
line in time. Furthermore it saves cutting off little bits of
line that have become worn.

In sketch No. 4 we have the end of the line teased out,
No. 5 shows the loop and the fuzzy end of the line waxed
and divided in three. Each of the three waxed parts is
threaded through the eye of a small needle and pushed
through the line. After the third one has been attended to
the whole splice is given a thorough waxing and then bound
with fly-tying silk the same colour as the line, a whip-finish
knot completes the job and we have the loop as drawing
No. 6.

Cast-Holder for Night Fishing

For those anglers who like fishing for sea-trout at night a
good idea is to make half a dozen cast-holders. They can be
constructed out of cardboard or celluloid and will prevent
getting tangled up when there is little or no light. Even the
light from an electric torch is not a satisfactory solution
when one has a tangled cast to unravel.

Another good point in favour of cast-holders is that they
enable the angler to make up a number of casts in advance.

A friend of mine makes his holders square-shaped, but I
much prefer them round.

The sketch will give the general idea how to make and
shape one.

Insect Repellent

During summer evenings flies can become a veritable
nuisance and in some cases these winged terrors can spoil
one's enjoyment. There are quite a number of good insect
repellents on the market, but I much prefer to make up my
own. Here's how:

From your chemist get 1 ounce of cedar oil; 2 ounces of
citronella oil and 2 ounces of spirits of camphor. Mix these
components by stirring in a glass jar and when thoroughly

mixed pour into small screw-topped containers and carry one whenever you go fishing. A few drops of the mixture rubbed into the skin of face, neck and hands will keep one immune for four to six hours.

If you prefer an ointment instead of a liquid insecticide, add a small jar of melted carbolated vaseline to the above formula and store your ointment in the vaseline jar or similar type of jar so long as it has a screw top.

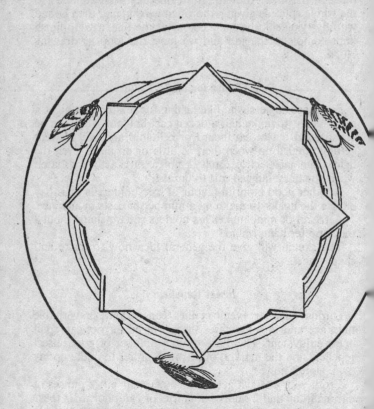

Easy to make Celluloid or Cardboard Cast Holder

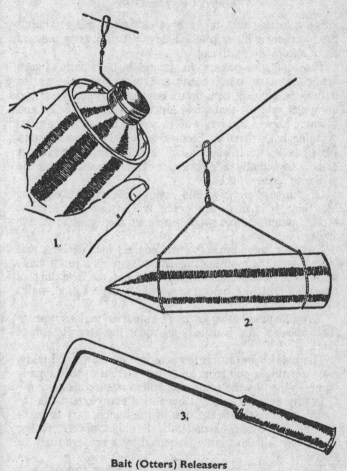

Bait (Otters) Releasers

1. Metal Polish Tin Otter   2. The Wye Otter
                3. Sand-eel Scraper

Always Carry an Otter

It's a shame that this age of electronic gadgets hasn't produced some little, infallible device for releasing snagged baits, natural and artificial.

The total loss per season, gauged in hard cash of such artificials as devons, spoons and plugs and mounts for natural baits, must be a pretty large sum. A few years ago an angler told me that while repairing a salmon lie he and the man he was working with recovered a number of metal spinning baits that had become wedged in between rocks. Now I believe that where a bait is lodged in between rocks or hooked actually on a rock, use of an otter will enable the angler to retrieve his bait.

Of course there is an old saying which goes something like this: 'It is an ill wind, etc.,' and in this case it is the tackle manufacturers who benefit at the expense of the angler.

However, there is another old adage which declares that 'necessity is the mother of invention,' and as a result many weird and wonderful contraptions, for the releasing of 'snagged' baits, have been invented by anglers in all walks of life.

Now like many other anglers I have tried various types of 'bait releases' which usually go under the general term of otter.

The majority work on the principle of submerged buoyancy creating a pull from an angle different to that already being applied by the angler himself to release his bait.

In fifty years of fishing I have tried many otters, but the two in the sketch are the best of the bunch, easy to make and the little energy expended by the angler in carrying one in his bag will invariably be repaid by a retrieved bait or two.

The sketches are fairly explanatory when coupled with the caption, but to make doubly sure here we go:

In the first drawing is an ordinary metal polish tin (empty of course) and with the lid screwed on tight. Round the neck is wound a piece of No. 12-gauge copper wire soldered to the tin neck and then shaped as per sketch and soldered to a link swivel. When the bait gets fast in rocks open the link swivel, put the contraption on the line and let slide down to where the bait is fast. Release a dozen or so yards of line so that it floats downstream, a few shakes of the rod top and usually the bait comes loose. Reel in, unhook the otter and away you go again.

The second otter in my opinion is the best of all round ones, being exceedingly light and easily made. The basic parts are an eight-inch tube of soldered tin or riveted aluminium, absolutely water-tight, three-inch diameter with one end cone-shaped.

Strong blind cord or cuttyhunk is used to fasten it to the swivel as per sketch. The length of cord at the cone end to swivel is the shorter and it is this end which must face where the bait is fast.

The method of handling is the same as the other otter referred to with one difference; with this otter the cone end must be kept pointing to the obstruction.

Either one of these bait releases can be made in less than an hour, but I feel quite sure that an otter will, during a season, save you a fair sum of money.

Sand-Eel Scraper

One of the best natural baits for early salmon is without a doubt an eel-tail. This bait is the tail half of the sand-eel and these silvery, eel-like fish are not always easy to come by. Granted one can purchase preserved ones from most tackle shops, but it has always been my experience that freshly caught baits lure better. There are two species of sand-eel (Launce) and the one most common round our coasts is the small-mouthed, which seldom exceeds seven or eight inches in length.

Wherever there is a sandy beach one can expect to find this excellent bait fish. As the tide recedes, the sand-eel by means of its under-protruding jaw and powerful body muscles is able to burrow into the wet sand out of reach of its many enemies, there to await the return of the sea.

Although they travel about in large shoals they are not always easy to find. The professional uses a fine-meshed seine net, but for the amateur who wants maybe a couple of dozen baits now and then, the purchase of a net would be money wasted. However, once you have located a sandy beach frequented by these fish it is, with the right tool, a comparatively easy matter to collect what you want.

For want of a better name I have called this tool a Sand-eel Scraper. It's over-all length is eighteen inches. The one I have used for over fifty years is made out of a twelve inch length of one-inch-rod steel which was shaped by a blacksmith friend in the days when there were plenty of horses about. The six-inch handle was fashioned from a piece of ordinary broom-shank.

Wait until low-water, then begin scraping in a zig-zag fashion, four to six inches below the surface of the sand near the water's edge. They settle in colonies and once you have uncovered one your task will be easy.

For salmon the bait wants to be from three to four inches in length, measuring from the tail, which means that the head and shoulders are removed. They can be preserved for about a fortnight in a strong solution of brine.

The sand-eel is also an excellent bait for bass, mackerel, pollack and coalfish, but for these sea fish the bait is best used alive.

Catching and Preserving Minnows

Throughout a trout season many good fish can be taken on minnow. I appreciate that one can purchase jars of these excellent baits, but there might come a time when a freshly caught bait is needed to outwit a good specimen. A trap is easy to make if one follows the simple instructions appended.

Materials and articles required are a piece of transparent celluloid, two-pound or one-pound clear glass jam jar, some rubber bands, a small piece of green muslin and a dozen paper studs, the sort that have pins that are pushed through and then bent over.

First job is to remove the bottom of the jar. A glass-cutter can do the removing quite easy but if there is not such a tool available then a piece of thick string soaked with petrol, tied round the jar at the point where you want the bottom removed, and ignited will answer nearly as well. After the string has burnt away a few taps with the wooden handle of a hammer or chisel will usually bring the bottom away quite clean.

The piece of muslin is cut to shape and fixed with a rubber band that must be a tight fit.

For the other end we make a cone out of the celluloid, the end which goes inside the jar having a hole just big enough to allow passage for the minnows. The other end should fit flush against the sides of the jar mouth. The paper studs can be put in and the cone is complete with the exception of three short pieces of rubber band which keep the cone in position. These are pinned and hang over the outside of the jar, another tight-fitting rubber band will hold these in place.

Some bread-crumbs or small worms are put in the jar, some cord is tied on and you are then ready to lower your trap into a place frequented by the little fish. Always have the cone-end (entrance) facing down-stream and it will not be long before you have a good supply of excellent baits.

For preserving minnows against the day when you cannot catch fresh ones use the same technique as that described for salmon baits in a previous paragraph.

20

SPOONS, DEVONS, MINNOWS AND WORM TACKLES

THERE never has been and possibly never will be a bait, natural or artificial, that will catch fish day in and day out in fresh or salt water. However, one that comes pretty near to such grading is the spoon. It will take, if properly used, coarse fish, fresh-water game fish and also sea fish. It has been in use since fishing began and oddly enough there are fewer competent spoon fishermen today than ever before. At least it would appear so because quite a number of tackle dealers have told me that they sell very few spoons nowadays.

Quite a few of the old-timers know its worth and year in and year out make good catches of salmon, sea-trout, trout, pike, perch and sea fish with it.

To give some idea of its antiquity I might mention that shortly before the last war I visited a Naples museum to see some ancient fishing tackle. There were relics of old flies, bone and ivory hooks and gorge tackles and also a number of spoons made of ivory, pearl shell and bone. The age of some of these baits, I was told, was over 2,000 years.

For my part I like the versatility of the spoon, for it can be used with the fly rod, spinning rod or short trolling rod. A friend of mine who is fortunate in that he does not have to work for a living, passes his time by fishing and throughout the entire salmon season he uses a spoon and, believe me, he catches plenty of salmon. In the early part of a season he uses the spinning rod and fishes deep, but from May until the season ends he works the spoon near the surface with an old 15-foot greenheart fly rod.

As a general artificial, the spoon is invaluable to the sea angler and will take fish throughout the whole year. Sometimes it will be bass, on another occasion pollack and during the summer months mackerel.

If you have no spoons in your kit take my advice and remedy the omission at once. They are easy to make and here is how I make mine:

From sheet copper of 1/32 inch thickness they are easy to shape. A piece of oak or other hard wood is obtained and

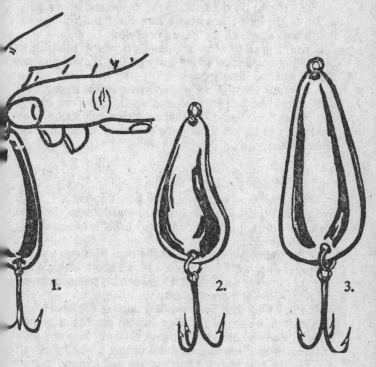

Some Home-made Spoons
1. Spoon for Trout and Sea-Trout 2. Salmon spoon
3. Spoon for Pike

the shape of the spoon you want is hollowed out with a gouge and smoothed with fine glass paper. A piece of the copper sheet is cut to the shape, placed in the hollow and tapped into shape with a small, round-headed hammer. Holes are drilled each end for split rings on which to put a hook and a swivel and the job is done. All that remains is to tin it with ordinary solder or paint it any colour your fancy dictates. If you tin the back of the spoon and give a good polish to the inside you have a nice silver and gold spoon. Polish both sides and you have a gold effect.

If you happen to know any jewellers you will be able to get hold of some sheet silver fairly reasonably and you can make some real silver spoons.

As to sizes you will not go far wrong if you stick to one half-inch to one inch for trout and sea-trout and one inch to two inches for salmon. For pike a three-inch spoon is an ideal size and for sea fishing one cannot do better than use salmon-size spoons.

Devons

About five years ago I was fishing that queen of English rivers, the Wye, and while doing so was initiated into the use of an artificial bait which it is my belief is not so widely used as it should be.

At the time I am speaking of the man who was using it was my ghillie, Mr. Elton Hussey. He was born within a few yards of the river and fishing it has been his sole occupation and recreation for more than fifty years.

As a boy Elton had been a willing pupil of the late Robert Pashley, the 'wizard of the Wye', whose records of salmon killed in a season are known the world over. So when such a fisherman as Elton Hussey declares that a wooden devon is one of the best baits for late summer and autumn salmon he is a wise man who takes notice.

However, being of a curious disposition my initiation started me wondering why a wood devon lured better than a metal one during the latter part of a season, so let us look at the pros and cons of metal versus wooden baits.

In the early part of a season we have to get the bait down due to the full state of the rivers and a metal one does the job well, but as the season advances waters become thin and with luxuriant weed growth near the bottom of most pools and streams.

Hooks pick up weed and valuable fishing time is expended in clearing them. Then again it has been my experience that salmon avoid a bait that has weeds streaming out behind it. To avoid weed the bait is brought through the water a little faster, but fast moving baits rarely catch fish; at least that is what I have found.

With a wooden bait the lead weight sinks, but the devon being buoyant, rises and travels on a horizontal course with a lively action no matter how slow the retrieve. While the lead might pick up a little weed the bait spins above it.

The depth at which you want the devon to work can be governed by the length of trace.

If it is a deep pool a foot or eighteen-inch trace will ensure the bait working within a few inches of the bottom. On streamy water where weeds can be pretty thick and where salmon delight to cruise during early morning and late evening a yard or four-foot trace will be found to answer best.

Apart from the foregoing advantages of light over heavy devons in the latter part of a season one must not forget the pleasure derived from making one's own baits. An evening can be profitably spent in fashioning half a dozen.

A four-foot length of round dowelling of half-inch diameter can be purchased from most furniture and joinery supply stores for a few new pence. The devons range in length from one and a half inches to two and a half inches. After being drilled they are shaped with a rough file and finished off with glass paper. The celluloid spinning vanes are inserted and twisted to shape in steam from a boiling kettle and all that remains is the colouring.

The colours which seem to attract late-run fish best are brown and gold, green and yellow and blue and silver.

Wood devons are light and take up very little room, so

why not make a few and give them a try when all else has failed to move a fish.

Metal devons are just as easy to make and they can be fashioned out of half-inch diameter copper or brass rod or even tubing. If you know someone who has a lathe it is a simple operation to get pieces of metal rod turned and drilled, otherwise it will have to be done by hand, but even then it need not be a long job once you get into the swing of things.

Quill Minnows

A fortnight before Christmas I pay a visit to a poultry-dealer fisherman friend of mine to collect a few strong primary feathers from the wings of geese and turkeys, with the quills from the best feathers I make some quill minnows.

This easy-to-make bait is a good one for early trout and for late evening sea-trout fishing from June to September.

In length these baits should range from two to three inches and the accompanying sketches illustrate, step by step, how to make them.

In drawing No. 1 is a quill with the fibres removed and in No. 2 we have a length of eight-pounds breaking strain nylon and a piece of plastic tubing which can be obtained from cheap ball-point pens. In No. 3 the tube has been inserted and the nylon runs through the tube. Give the tube a thin coat of clear nail varnish on the outside so that it will stick to the quill at the hook end. The head of the quill has been notched for the spinning vanes (celluloid) which are shaped as in sketch No. 4.

In the last drawing we see the completed quill minnow. The small treble hook has had the nylon bound on with waxed fly-tying silk, the spinning vanes are in place and the swivel has been tied in at the head which has been filled round the plastic tube with plastic wood. While the wood is moist bind the notches into place with nylon thread and give it a couple of coats of clear nail varnish. When dry the minnow can be coloured on the back to represent a young trout or other immature fish. Leave the underside in its

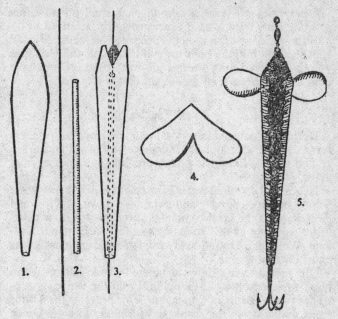

Making Quill Minnows
1. Turkey Quill with feather removed
2. Wire and plastic tube
3. Quill shaped with nylon and tube through centre
4. Shape of celluloid spinning vanes
5. Completed minnow

natural colour. When the paint on the back is perfectly dry give it a coat of good-grade clear copal varnish and the job is done.

Some quill minnows I have seen offered for sale have a couple of additional treble hooks, one near the middle of the bait and the other at the head. However, it has been my experience that one treble at the tail is best, extra hooks tend to throw the bait off balance as it is coming through the water.

I have never caught a salmon on a quill minnow, but several of my friends have when fishing for sea-trout.

If the water you fish is on the deep side half a dozen small split shot put into the body around the plastic tube will give you the required weight to get the bait down, otherwise the plastic wood head is all the weight that is required.

Worm Tackles

During the course of every salmon and trout season there comes a time when our old friend the worm will take a fish or two when all else has failed, providing, of course, rules allow.

Heavy and coloured water is just right for ordinary worm fishing such as ledgering and swimming down, and low and clear water is the ideal combination for up-stream or clear-water worming as it is sometimes called. In England, Scotland, Wales and Ireland many salmon are caught each year on a bunch of worms.

Our first drawing shows a tapered-shank salmon worm hook whipped on to 12-lb. nylon. From the whipping protrudes two whiskers of 8-lb. nylon. This prevents the worms from sliding down the shank and forming too big a bunch at the hook bend and the barb. It was on the River Teify, many years ago, that I saw this type of worm hook in operation. It certainly is an advance on the old type of plain whipped hook. Of course in some types of hooks, notably sea hooks, the shanks have two or three small barbs up the shank which answer the same purpose.

Drawing No. 2 is of a single round bend hook for trout or sea-trout and as a safety measure against the hook pulling out a simple knot has been tied in the 6-lb. nylon before it is whipped to the shank.

In No. 3 we have Pennell (two-hook) tackle which is in great demand by up-stream trout anglers. Sometimes the pair of hooks are in line with each other, but some fishermen prefer the second hook in position as per the dotted-line hook.

In the last sketch is Stewart tackle (three hooks) and here

the middle hook can be in line or as the dotted-line hook. This type of worm tackle is also used extensively for upstream work, particularly in Scotland.

In the making of all worm tackles it is advisable to give the hook shank a thin coat of clear nail varnish and then a winding of red fly-dressing silk. This makes a good foundation for the nylon and the whipping. I have experimented with all manner of whipping materials and have come to the opinion that ordinary red fly-dressing silk, well waxed, is the best. After the hook or hooks are whipped to the nylon

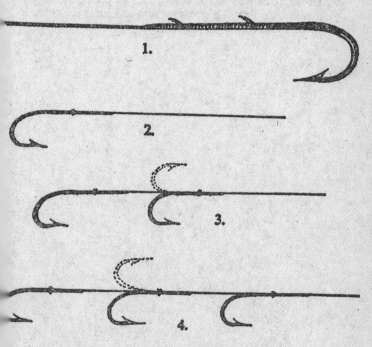

Worm Tackles

1. Worm hook for Salmon
2. Worm hook for Trout
3. Pennell Tackle
4. Stewart Tackle

a coat of clear nail varnish is essential to prevent the binding becoming frayed from use.

The length of nylon bound to the hook is a matter of fancy, it can be a foot, two feet or a yard. I compromise and make all mine two feet. A fly-dressing vice assists considerably in holding the hook, thus leaving both hands free.

Of course if you do not want to bother making up your own tackle most tackle shops now sell brazed Pennell tackle. The two hooks are on one shank, but such a tackle is very hard on worms as in their wriggling they get torn and soon die. The tackle made at home with the nylon link joining the two hooks gives way to the contortions of the creature.

However, for dressing streamer flies and lures the brazed Pennell answers very well.

21

CREATING ARTIFICIAL JUNGLE COCK

W HEN fly dressers both amateur and professional were unable to purchase jungle cock feathers the question asked was usually, 'Why this shortage?''

The answer is simple. Jungle cock not only provides beautiful feathers, but it is also good to eat as I know from first-hand experience.

Years ago they used to roam certain Indian jungles in their hundreds of thousands, but so great was their slaughter for food and the feather trade that the species were in danger of becoming extinct. To try and save them a Government ban was placed on the export of skins.

As a journalist I was in India in 1932 and could have purchased skins for the equivalent of 10 new pence each, they were so plentiful.

However, "necessity" we are often told "is the mother of invention," and it was not long before ideas on the creation of substitutes were forthcoming. I have tried many such and I give here what I consider to be the two best.

For making large substitutes you need some black cock hackles. The fluff at the base of the feather is removed as per sketch No. 1. The tip of the feather is then made round with a pair of scissors and the white, waxy looking eyes of real jungle cock is made by applying white plastic paint to the feather.

I have found that the best way to do this is to file the round head of a nail until it is oval in shape. The paint is placed on this and then dabbed on the feather. See sketch No. 2.

Half-a-dozen different sized nails filed to shape will enable

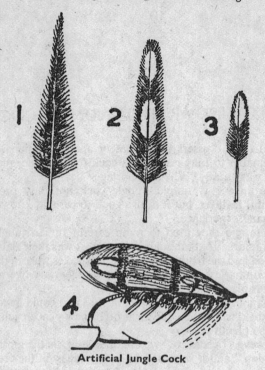

Artificial Jungle Cock

you to make up different sizes of eyes in your substitutes. It takes a little practice, but eventually you will get the hang of it.

In sketch No. 3 we have a different type of feather, it is from the breast of a cock starling. Skins of these birds can be purchased from most tackle dealers. Remove the fluff as before and touch the tip with white plastic paint.

The tip of a feather from a cock starling is a natural dirty white in colour and the plastic paint emphasises this.

Treated in this way starling feathers are ideal for trout, sea trout and rainbow trout flies and when very small salmon flies are needed for summer periods of low water, such as No. 8 or 10 they can be used for these also.

In the last sketch No. 4 is a Durham Ranger salmon fly, which normally would have needed four Jungle cock feathers, but has been made with substitutes.

A friend of mine who fishes the River Test for salmon has had, over the last three seasons, excellent results with flies dressed with substitute jungle cock.

I am convinced that in the very near future more and more substitutes for certain feathers will have to be found as natural supplies become more difficult to obtain each year. Many breeds of domestic poultry that provided feathers for trout flies are just a memory, but science has provided dyes and with these the feather trade has been able to create excellent replacements.

22

SOME NEW FLIES

Over the last ten years so great has been the increase in numbers of fly fishermen that man-made lakes and even streams are being created where-ever suitable places can be found. Today fly fishing for trout is very big business.

But the new waters are not the sole preserve of brown trout for over the years it has been found rainbow trout grow much faster than browns and further more the former species are not so prone to disease.

Of course rainbow trout are nothing new to this country; the Bristol Waterworks have been stocking their reservoirs with them for a great many years.

The famous River Test in Hampshire, once famous for its wild brown trout, now has its quota of rainbows.

In the wake of this change-over from browns to rainbows we have had a flood of new fly patterns on the market, particularly in nymphs, for a rainbow is not such a free-riser as the brown. The former is a native of America and a good many patterns used over there are now on sale in this country, so here are a few together with sketches of what I consider to be the more important ones.

The Black Creeper

This fly was invented in America some years ago, but it has done exceedingly well in this country where ever it has been tried.

In our first sketch we have the hook, a long-shank No. 10 in the vice, a length of black wool is waiting to be wound

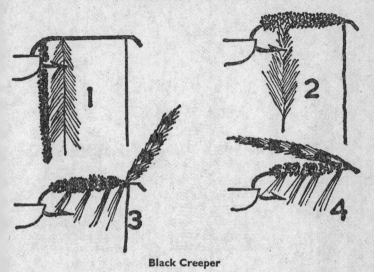

Black Creeper

round the shank and also we have a badger hackle, tied in by its tip, this will rib the body.

Drawing No. 2 sees the black body in place, and in No. 3 the badger hackle has been wound round and the feather filaments on top have been cut off. A well-marked Plymouth Rock cock hackle is tied in by its base and we see the finished fly in No. 4.

If you have any difficulty in obtaining Plymouth Rock hackle feathers it is fairly easy to make your own for all you need is a plain white hackle feather and one of those large felt-tipped black ink marking pens. They are sold at most stationers and stores. The best kind is that which has an oblique cut point as it marks the feather much better, you can also vary the depth of your marks, see sketches.

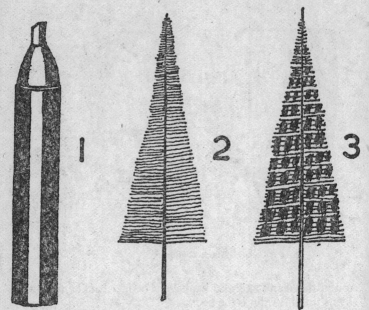

Making an artificial Plymouth Rock Hackle

Rubber-band Nymph

This pattern also originated in America and has proved its worth when both brown and rainbow trout are foraging on the bed of a stream or chasing nymphs as they rise to the surface of stream and lake prepartory to changing into fly proper.

At most stores and stationers you can purchase for a few pence a packet of rubber bands of mixed colours and sizes, this enables one to create artificials with different coloured bodies.

In our first sketch a No. 10 hook is being used and a tail of half-a-dozen fibres from a Rhode Island cock hackle has been tied in well down the hook bend. A strip from the wing

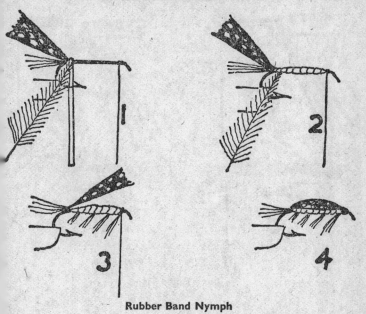

Rubber Band Nymph

feather of a guinea fowl is tied in just above the tail, this will form the back. In front of this is a small badger hackle which when wound round the body forms the legs. Next we have a narrow gauge rubber band, that has been cut to make it one piece.

The next sketch has the body complete and in No. 3 the hackle is wound round and trimmed as per sketch. We have the finished nymph in No. 4.

For the use of friends and self I make these nymphs up in three sizes: 8, 10 and 12.

Long-tailed Tit

This is a British fly and is used pretty extensively on lakes and reservoirs for both browns and rainbows and is usually

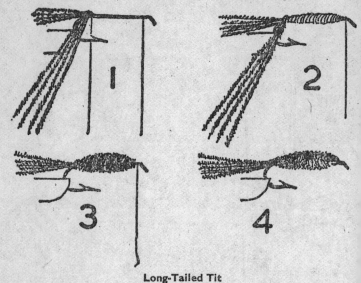

Long-Tailed Tit

equipped with a weighted body made of either fine lead or copper wire. The dressing given here is weighted.

In the first drawing a tail composed of half-a-dozen strands of bronze peacock herl has been tied in. The tail should be at least half an inch in length. Four strands of similar herl is tied in and left hanging, these will form the body. A length of fine copper wire is also ready to be wound and the tying silk has been wound back to near the hook eye.

In the following drawing the copper wire has been wound in and the surplus cut off. In No. 3 the body is complete and in our last sketch we have the finished pattern.

Some long-tailed tits I have seen have bodies made of white, green and orange coloured wools and the peacock herl is tied in on top to form the back.

Whichever type of long-tailed tit you dress you will find it very easy to make.

Gilbert Caterpillar

This pattern was invented about ten years ago by a then
Hampshire New Forest Ranger, now retired, and known to
all his friends as Gilbert.

One day Gilbert was fishing a pool on the Lymington
River, Hampshire, but failed to rise a fish although brown
trout and sea trout were rising all round him.

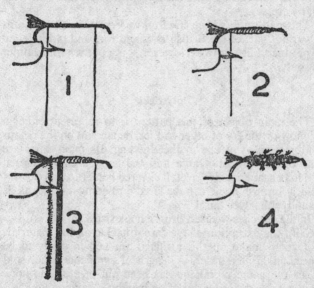

Gilbert Caterpillar

Then he noticed a number of small green caterpillars
hanging by their silken threads from the bushes and trees
that over-hung the pool. At home that night he set about
creating an artificial green caterpillar. Here is the dressing.

In our first sketch a tuft of green wool has been tied in as
a tail and hanging next to it is a length of 15 amp. fuse wire
to give the pattern weight to sink. The green tying silk has
been wound to near the hook eye.

In No. 2 the fuse wire has been wound and the tying silk has been wound back to the hook bend. In the following sketch a length of green peacock herl and one of pale green wool is fastened.

The last sketch illustrates the finished pattern with the peacock herl ribbing the body. Incidentally the green peacock herl is obtained from the sword feather from the peacock and can be purchased from tackle dealers catering for fly dressers.

This pattern has been tried on waters, lakes and streams in various part of the British Isles and Eire and rarely failed to produce a fish or two. However, it is a pattern for summer use only.

Polystickle

The main object of this pattern is to represent either a minnow or the fry of other species, dependant on the colour combinations you use in the dressing. Its main parts are plastic and synthetic raffia and the hook used is silvered and long shanked. However, if silvered hooks are not obtainable a bronze hook can be used providing the shank is wound with silver tinsel.

In the sketches we use a bronze hook size 8.

With the exception of the throat hackle all the materials that go to make up this artificial are tied in ready to be placed in proper order. A length of synthetic raffia, sold under the name of raffene has been put in near the hook bend with about a quarter of an inch over-hanging which is cut square to represent a tail. Next there is a length of polythene about .005 inch thick, next to this is a length of silver tinsel. The black tying silk has been wound to near the hook eye and here a little red wool has been wound, two turns is quite sufficient; the tying silk is then fastened off nearer the eye.

In No. 2 the silver tinsel is in position and the following sketch shows how the shape of the raffene should look after it is wound. It should have the shape of a little fish and the

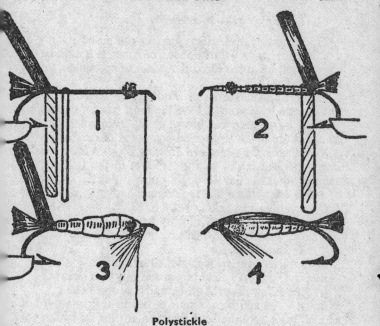

Polystickle

clearer the polythene the better it will look, as the silver tinsel and red wool will show through.

The throat hackle can be bright yellow, orange, black or red. The throat hackle is in position in No. 3 and we have the finished polystickle in No. 4, with the raffene forming the back.

One point to remember when building the body is that as you wind, stretch the polythene a little particularly when changing direction. This ensures a smooth finish.

A coat of clear nail varnish on the raffene makes it glisten when moving about in the water, and should be put on after you have finished dressing it.

Muddler Fly

This strangely named creation is composed mainly of deer hair and among the rainbows of America it must be the most feared for it has lured thousands of specimens, to end finally in the pan.

There is a whole series of Muddlers of differing colours, but the one with which I have the most success on various waters I have fished has brown as the main colour and its main feature is the large head composed of deer hair.

Here then is the American dressing. Reason for emphasising American is due to the fact that in the British Isles many fly-dressers have brought out many variations, some of which are nothing like the original design.

Hook: Long-shank either No. 8 or 10.

Tail: Half-inch length of grey turkey and half an inch wide, doubled and then tied in. With it some fibres of deer hair a little longer.

Body: Silver tinsel, ribbed oval silver tinsel.

Wings: Grey turkey and brown and grey deer hair.

Hackle: A few fibres of brown and grey deer hair.

Body, wings and hackle must be tied in at least a third of an inch back from the hook eye, to allow for the making of the large head which is composed of small bunches of grey deer hair. As each bunch is tied in it will flair round like the spokes of a wheel. It usually takes about four such bunches to make the head. When complete cut the hair short and you will have a fly, which when in the water looks like a minnow.

Jersey Herd

This is another modern fly for brown or rainbow trout invented by Mr. T. Ivens who did so much to popularise reservoir fishing for the above two species. It is a colourful example of the fly dresser's art, but what it is supposed to represent is anyone's guess. However the fact remains it does attract and catch fish. There are quite a few variations in the dressing of this pattern, but here is the original dressing.

Hook: No. 6, 8 or 10 long-shank.

Tail: Half a dozen fibres of bronze peacock herl.

Body: This is built up to the shape of a small fish with floss silk or fine wool and covered with copper tinsel.

Hackle: This is made from a cock hackle dyed bright orange.

Back: This is composed of seven or eight fibres of bronze peacock herl which over-laps the back of the copper tinsel.

Head: Made of bronze peacock herl, three or four turns is quite enough.

The variations mentioned above usually have silver or gold bodies and green peacock herl back and tail.

Worm Fly

This is not a new fly but so many readers of the first edition of this book requested its dressing, hence the reason for its inclusion.

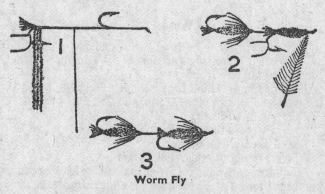

Worm Fly

In the old days we joined two hooks sizes No. 8, 10 or 12 together with natural gut, then along came nylon and now you can purchase two hooks in tandem brazed on one shank and for the dressing of a worm fly the combination is ideal.

The first sketch has the end hook in the vice and a tail of

fibres from a red feather is in place and hanging down are
three strands of bronze peacock herl.

With illustration No. 2 the herl has been wound on and a
Rhode Island cock hackle has been put on thus completing
the first half of the fly. The second hook has been placed in
the vice and the same procedure is repeated.

In No. 3 we have the fly complete.

It is an excellent pattern for both brown trout and rainbows, but for work in reservoirs and deep pools it often pays
to add a little weight before the dressing is put on by winding
on a little fine copper or lead wire. I have often used a
weighted worm fly at the start of a season when fish are
hunting for food near the bottom. In streams just clearing
after a flood it usually pays to give it a try before using any
other pattern.

Most tackle dealers stock these brazed hooks, but should
you have difficulty in obtaining them they can be obtained
from E. Veniard, Ltd., 138, Northwood Road, Thornton
Heath, Surrey.

Whisky Fly

This modern fly is both colourful and has a delightful
name, what is more it has accounted for salmon, sea trout,
brown and rainbow trout.

The dressing is, Hook for reservoir fishing No. 8 and 10,
for river and stream No. 12. Salmon sizes, No. 4 and 6.

Tail: Small red feather.

Body: Flat gold tinsel, ribbed oval gold tinsel.

Throat hackle: Hot orange.

Wings: Four hot-orange cock hackles.

A hot-orange dye for colouring plain white hackles can be
purchased for a few pence from most tackle dealers.

Lures and Streamer Flies

Coinciding with the growth of reservoir and lake, now
known as still-water fishing, there has been an increase in

the number of lure and streamer patterns. For the former
the brazed tandem (Pennell) hooks already mentioned are
ideal. The streamer fly is of course dressed on a long-shanked
hook. .

The lure has always been a firm favourite with sea trout
anglers operating along estuaries, but in the last few years it
has come into its own among still-water fishermen.

How to dress both lure and streamer was given in an
earlier chapter and I give here only a few of the newer
designs invented mostly by amateur fly dressers.

I used my first lure for brown trout about 60 years ago in
the mountain streams of North Wales. They were dressed
on small hooks No. 14 and 16 and were deadly in those fast
waters particularly after a flood.

The streamer is an all-purpose fly and can be used in all
types of water for members of the game fish family.

Here then are the dressings of the more modern ones,
with lures first.

Magpie

I first saw this pattern being used at Chew, one of Bristol
Waterworks reservoirs:

Tail: Golden pheasant tippet fibres.
Body: This is in two parts, the end hook has a body of
   black ostrich herl and the other has the body made of
   white wool with both being ribbed with fine oval silver
   tinsel.
Hackle: Fibres of blue jay.
Wings: Four black cock hackles, extending to the end of
   the tail.

Orange and Red

A colourful example of the fly dresser's art.
Tail: Golden pheasant topping feather, and a few fibres
   of golden pheasant tippet.

Body: Both hooks have bodies made of fluorescent orange
   wool ribbed with oval silver tinsel.
Throat hackle: Red cock.
Wings: First a half-inch strip from a dyed swan feather
   over which is placed a broad strip of bronze mallard so
   that the red shows along the body. A variation is that
   instead of mallard one can use a well-marked teal or
   widgeon feather from which to take the strip.

Teal and Blue

This is an excellent sea trout pattern.
Tail: Fibres of golden pheasant tippet.
Body: Bright blue floss silk the whole length and ribbed
   with oval silver tinsel.
Throat hackle: Black cock.
Wings: Broad strip of teal with artificial jungle cock on
   cheeks. Of course if you have natural jungle cock put
   these on by all means.

White Queen

As its name suggests this is a white lure which when the
body is weighted with fine copper or lead wire has proved
its worth on many still waters all over the country.
Tail: Golden pheasant tippet.
Body: The whole length is white fluorescent wool ribbed
   with flat silver tinsel.
Throat hackle: Bright orange.
Wings: Four plain white cock hackles, reaching to end of
   the tail. Jungle cock cheeks.

Mallard and Black

This is a good all-round pattern for brown, rainbow and
sea trout.
Tail: Golden pheasant topping.
Body: The whole shank is black floss silk ribbed oval
   silver tinsel.

Throat hackle: Bright orange.
Wings: Broad strip of bronze mallard with jungle cock
cheeks.

Teal and Green

This is another all-purpose pattern and has been known
to lure a salmon or two.
Tail: Golden pheasant topping with a few fibres of golden
pheasant tippet.
Body: Green floss silk the whole length ribbed oval gold
tinsel.
Wings: Broad strips of well-marked teal.
Hackle: This is placed ahead of the wings and is wound
to form a sort of collar and can be bright yellow or
orange.
All the lures I have described are dressed on No. 8 or 10
hooks.

Streamers

About 50 years ago I saw my first streamer fly, it was in
British Columbia and was being used by a journalist col-
league. I was so intrigued by its success against the Kamloop
rainbows that on my return to this country I wrote about
luring qualities and also did three broadcasts from the old
B.B.C. studio, in Bridge Street, Newcastle-on-Tyne.

I am still of the same opinion I formed those many years
ago and that is, the streamer fly is one of the finest designs
ever created, for the downfall of game fish.

In the U.S.A. large streamer flies are in use now for luring
salt-water gamesters like Tarpon, Albacore, Wahoo, Bone-
fish and several others.

Here then are half a dozen pattern that will be new to
many anglers of this country, but are always worth dressing
and giving a try-out.

Chief Needabeh

No tail.
Body: Scarlet floss silk, ribbed oval silver tinsel.
Wings: Two orange cock hackles tied over two yellow
  hackles, the orange hackles being a little shorter in
  length.
Throat hackle: Yellow and scarlet hackle fibres mixed.

York's Kennebago

No tail.
Body: Silver tinsel, ribbed oval tinsel.
Wings: Four badger hackles.
Cheeks: Jungle cock.
Head hackle: Scarlet kept short.

Gootenburg's Jersey Minnow

Tail: Golden pheasant tippet fibres.
Body: Gold tinsel, ribbed oval gold tinsel.
Wings: Two badger hackles.
Throat hackle: Ginger feather fibres mixed with pink, with
  a head of green peacock herl.

Estelle

Tail: Scarlet feather fibres.
Body: Alternate scarlet and white chenille ribbed with
  gold oval tinsel.
Wings: Two plain white cock hackles with two small red
  feathers one on each cheek.
Throat hackle: White feather fibres.

Fraser

No tail or throat hackle.
Body: Green wool, ribbed oval silver tinsel, with a tuft of
  scarlet wool at the bend of the hook.

Wings: Two plain white cock hackles with two shorter yellow cock hackles.
Cheeks: Jungle cock.

Scott Special

Tail: Scarlet feather fibres.
Body: Light brown wool, ribbed oval silver tinsel.
Wings: Four yellow cock hackles.
Cheeks: Jungle cock.
Throat hackle: Bright yellow or orange feather fibres.
   Hooks are always long shank No. 4, 6, 8, 10 or 12.

Hair-Wing Flies

Like streamers, flies wings composed of hair were first invented and used in the U.S.A. and Canada and date back hundreds of years long before hooks made of metal were ever thought of. Today, in the British Isles we have hundreds of patterns with hair wings. In the realm of the dry-fly purist we have the hair-winged Mayfly patterns invented by American Lee Woolf.

I have a friend who is an expert with a nymph and he makes these out of real leopard hair. His pattern has accounted for scores of large rainbows up to 9 lbs. He fishes a stream which issues from the River Test.

Here then is half a dozen of hair winged flies that have proved their worth all over the country.

Black Bucktail

An excellent fly for all kinds of trout and a friend of mine has had three salmon on it when sea trout fishing in Scotland.

With all hair-wing flies it is always advisable to give the roots of the hair, before tying in, a dab of clear nail varnish or some kind of adhesive to seal them tight and then fasten them in place while still sticky. Unless this precaution is

taken the hairs will work loose and start to fall out. The
dressing is as follows : -

Tail: Red, orange or yellow feather fibres.

Body: Black floss silk, ribbed with flat or oval silver tinsel.

Wings: Black bucktail hairs, bunched together, but err on
the sparse side or when you come to make whip finish
at the head it will be much too bulky and will look
unsightly.

Throat hackle: Blue jay feather fibres.

Cheeks: Jungle cock.

Salmon Bucktail

An excellent pattern for salmon particulary grilse and also
sea trout when they are in sea pools or estuaries. It is most
useful when late evening and night fishing; however, it works
best in this period if the mixed coloured hairs have been
treated with fluorescent dyes.

The dressing:-

Tail: Golden pheasant topping.

Body: This is in two halves, the first being black floss silk
and the second is red floss silk, the whole body being
ribbed with oval silver tinsel.

Throat hackle: Black and blue jay feather fibres mixed.

Wings: A sparse bunch of black bucktail, next a smaller
one of red and the third bright yellow.

Cheeks: Jungle cock.

Bucktail Prawn

This is a favourite pattern with many friends of mine and
has accounted for a good many summer run salmon.

Tail: About a dozen bucktail fibres, dyed red and extending over the bend of the hook for at least one inch.

Body: First tie in a sparse bunch of red and orange bucktail to form the back or shell, next tie in an orange red
cock hackle. The body is then made of red floss silk,
ribbed with flat gold tinsel and the hackle is wound,

palmer fashion to near the eye. The last operation is to bring the red and orange bucktail over the top and it is tied off in the usual way.

Hackle fibres that are protruding out from the sides should be trimmed off.

The head should be red varnish.

Yellow Bucktail

A pattern that is always worth a try in coloured water or just as the water is clearing after a flood when one is after salmon or sea trout.

Tail: Golden pheasant tippet fibres.
Body: Gold floss silk ribbed flat gold tinsel.
Throat hackle: Bright orange cock hackle fibres.
Wings: Bright yellow bucktail.
Cheeks: Jungle cock.

Squirrel Tail

There are many variations of this pattern, but each has wings composed of grey squirrel tail hairs. While I have taken many sea trout on it I have yet to lure a salmon.

No tail.
Body: Black floss silk ribbed oval silver tinsel.
Throat hackle: Blue jay feather fibres.
Wings: Small bunch of grey squirrel tail hair.
The dressing above is the one I have used mostly.

Yellow Squirrel Tail

This is dressed in the same way as above with the one exception, the wings have been dyed a bright fluorescent yellow.

Hair is also useful for making lures and the one I was never without when fishing a reservoir, loch or Irish lake was the Black and Peacock. This pattern is usually dressed with feather wings and bronze peacock herl body. The hair-winged variety is made with green peacock herl and black deer hair wings, a bright orange throat hackle, and jungle cock cheeks.

It is my belief that in the very near future we shall have to rely more and more on hair for our fly wings due to the shortage of bird plumage.

The size of hooks for hair-winged patterns are the same as if the wings were of feathers.

A New Body Material

There is now on the market a new material for making bodies and like so many things associated with angling it was first used in the U.S.A.

It is a plastic foil but looks like ordinary metal tinsel and has one great advantage over ordinary tinsel in that it does not tarnish when used in brackish (estuary) waters or in the sea. Its trade name is "Mylar" and it can be plain or embossed, in strips, or piping.

However, the one I have used most in dressing is the piping which is just a tube of Mylar but is braided and this criss-cross appearance gives the body of a fly the appearance of having scales. It is most useful for salmon and sea trout flies, lures and streamers.

It can be purchased in small, medium or large sizes.

All you have to do to give a fly a small fish appearance is cut off the length of piping you require, take out the string core around which the Mylar is braided and then slip the resultant tube over the hook eye and along the shank. If it is too slack build up to fit the tube with floss silk or fine wool, give this a coating of clear nail varnish and then put on your little tube. Both ends should be tied in to stop them from fraying, you then proceed with your dressing as usual.

Tube flies that are dressed with this material are most attractive.

If you do any sea fishing for mackerel or pollack you will find that a Mylar bodied hook will attract these two species

Mylar Tube Mackerel Lure

much more than that well-known lure, commonly called "feathers".

To make a salt-water lure is simplicity itself, all you do is build up the hook-shank as already suggested, slip on the tube and tie off both ends and the job is complete. When worked sink and draw it looks like a little fish, and if you use four or more on the leader you can alternate the colours one silver the other gold.

To my way of thinking Mylar is a most useful and versatile material and one no fly-dresser should be without. I like a tail on my mackerel lures; all you do is get a pin or needle and unbraid the strands before tying in as per sketch No. 4.

23

MORE NEW PATTERNS

I THINK most people, whether they be anglers or not, will agree that a well-dressed pattern, whatever type it may be is an amalgam of beauty and craftsmanship. Many of the recent additions are most colourful. What is more they do interest members of the Salmo family and, after all, that is the one qualification we fly-fishermen are interested in.

Many veteran anglers will notice in some of the new flies only slight variations from much older patterns. The fact remains, however, that in many cases, the change has improved the luring qualities of that particular fly.

It would take several volumes to detail each new fly invented by amateurs and professionals in the last few years. However, the ones mentioned in this chapter have been thoroughly tested, over a long period, not only by the author and his family, but by many friends throughout the British Isles. They include lures, streamers and nymphs.

When I started fly-fishing there were no weighted nymphs. Now most are made to sink, some more rapidly than others. Furthermore we now have floating nymphs, and such patterns are most deadly during the start of an evening rise as I have proved time and again.

Woodcock and Blue Lure

A lure on which my wife has caught many fine rainbows is one designed and tied by her about five years ago. I have never mentioned it before, the simple reason being that before one can recommend a particular artificial it must have undergone a severe testing period. This pattern has been through that period. It was fully tested on waters in my own country Wales, Scotland, Ireland and England in both still and running water. In 1977 my eldest daughter Sylvia gave it a good try-out in British Columbia among the giant Kamloop rainbow trout and did quite well. Her guide suggested using 'hard-ware' like spoons, plugs and devons, but persevering with her mother's pattern she out-caught her mentor by three fish.

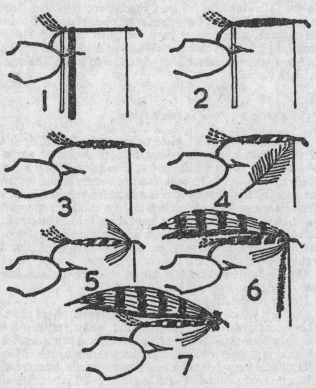

Woodcock and blue lure

In Scotland the same year Sylvia had nine sea trout in four hours fishing, the largest being 6½ lbs.

Here is the dressing and key to the sketches:—

In No. 1 we have a No. 8 long-shank hook in the vice. A tail of golden pheasant fibres is tied in for the tail and left hanging are lengths of flat silver tinsel and light blue floss silk. With No. 2 the hook shank has been wound with the silk floss, and in No. 3 the silk has been ribbed with the tinsel. In No. 4 a blue coloured hackle feather is tied in and in the following sketch it is wound, three turns are quite enough. With No. 6 the wings, composed of strips from a woodcock's wing feather have been tied in along with a length of green peacock herl. We have the finished pattern in No. 7 with the peacock herl wound into place. The head is black varnish.

Taylor's Pride

One of Hampshire's leading tackle dealers' was Taylor's of Christchurch, the proprietor being a dedicated angler and designer of flies, Bill Taylor, who passed away a few years ago. However, he will always be remembered as the inventor of the Green Nymph which he named Taylor's Pride. It is a very simple pattern to dress and has accounted for some very large rainbows and brown trout. The largest Bill ever caught was a 9 lb. rainbow from a side stream of the River Test, at Romsey. He also had many fine brown trout over 6 lbs.

On a long-shaped hook it can be dressed as a lure and is a useful change pattern on still water.

Here is the dressing:—

Our first sketch of this useful nymph has the tail in place. This is composed of fibres from the breast feather of a golden pheasant. A strip of heron from a wing feather which is grey coloured is tied in along with a length of fine oval gold tinsel and one of bright green floss silk. Sketch No. 2 has the body complete and in No. 3 a throat hackle of fibres, the same as the tail is in position. We see the finished

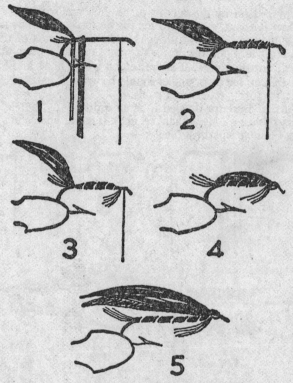

Taylor's pride nymph and lure

pattern in No. 5. It is also useful in deep water when
weighted and this can be achieved by putting on the shank
some fine lead or copper wire before the body material.

To make the lure a No. 8 or No. 10 long-shank hook is
used and the heron feather strips should extend half-an-
inch over the tail. This lure is a reasonably good change
pattern when after sea trout in estuaries near the sea.

Barbara's Special

Spurred on by the success of her husband's pattern his widow Barbara, who now runs the business, experimented with many of her own designs and after months of trial and error hit upon the design of what I might be permitted to call a real winner. It is dressed on a keel hook and is a lure that no sea trout angler should be without particularly when exploring estuary sea pools.

At first Barbara dressed it as an ordinary fly, but later decided with a longer shanked hook it could be used as a lure. First we will dress the fly:—

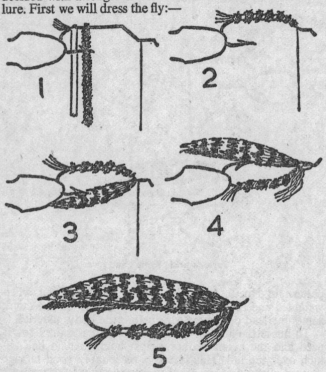

Barbara's special fly and lure on keel hooks

In the first sketch is a No. 10 keel fly hook, on which we have a tail of golden pheasant topping feather tied in, a length of flat silver tinsel and one of several fibres of bronze peacock herl, twisted together. The body is complete in drawing No. 2 and in the following sketch the wings composed of teal drake strips are tied in. To complete the fly the hook is changed over so that the hook point is uppermost and the throat hackle of golden pheasant topping fibres is in place, thus completing the fly, as in No. 4.

The same procedure is adopted when tying the lure on a No. 8 or No. 6 hook as depicted in No. 5.

Keith Hall's Streamer

This hair-wing pattern is a most excellent pattern for sea trout, but it has also proved its worth on various types of water where brown and rainbow trout are present. I first met Keith on a well stocked water in Hampshire. He had taken his limit of four fish in a couple of hours, and quite naturally I was curious as to the fly he had used. Not only did he show me the fly but gave me one and I had my limit by tea-time. I have used it many times since and found it to be all that Keith claimed for it.

On the Hampshire rivers Avon and Stour it has taken many fine sea trout, hence it is included in this chapter.

The dressing is as follows:—

The first sketch has a No. 8 long-shank hook in the vice and a tail of red ibis is tied in and lengths of flat silver tinsel and black wool are waiting to be wound. The tying silk has been wound to near the hook eye. In No. 2 the wool has been tied in and with No. 3 the body is complete. The wings of black deer or squirrel hair are in place in No. 4. However remember to put on a little clear varnish on the roots of the hair before tying in. This simple procedure will prevent the hairs from becoming loose when the fly is in use. The next drawing has a hackle of fibres from a red hackle tied in along with a length of bronze peacock herl. With No. 6 we have the finished pattern with

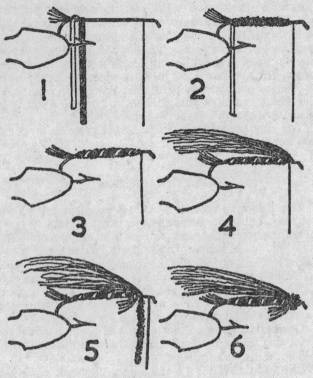

Keith Hall's streamer

a head of three turns of the bronze herl and the final whip
finish being of black varnish.

Tandem Minnow

Along with the growth of new artificials there has been
a real spate of weird and wonderful shaped hooks. Having

dealt with one new type, the keel hook, here is another that I first came across as representing an artificial minnow. On a long shanked hook had been brazed a second hook facing upwards. In the old days, as I have mentioned elsewhere in an earlier chapter we had to link hooks together with silk-worm gut and later on with nylon. Now the whole business is simplified.

It was on the River Tavy, Devon, during an autumn run of sea trout, the pools were full of fish, but my take during

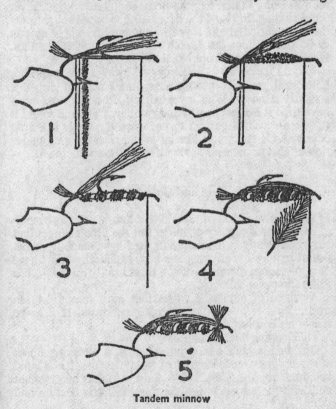

Tandem minnow

three hours hard fishing was only three fish. My host, Col. Langdale who was following me had taken nine beautiful specimens, the largest 9 lbs. Over a glass of good malt whisky he showed me the pattern that had lured them, and here is the dressing:—

With No. 1 sketch a tail of golden pheasant topping fibres has been tied in and lengths of flat silver tinsel and green peacock herl are hanging. On top is a bunch of black deer hair. In No. 2 the peacock herl has been wound and the following sketch has the body complete with its silver tinsel ribbing. In No. 4 the deer hair has been brought over the top and tied in and a yellow coloured hackle is waiting to be wound. Our last sketch reveals the finished pattern. Hooks range in size from No. 8 to No. 12.

My old friend the Colonel passed away a few years ago, but I shall never forget the first time I met up with this artificial minnow. Who invented it I do not know, but I have tried it against brown and rainbow trout and found it to be an excellent pattern to use when the water is a little coloured. On still water like lakes and reservoirs a foundation of lead or copper wire enables it to get well down.

Teal and Gold Lure

This is a variation of the old teal lure which has been in existence for a century or more, but the little changes that have been made in the materials used have made it a most useful pattern for any angler's box. My family and I have not only taken members of the trout family on it but also grilse (first year salmon).

A friend of ours who fishes that most famous of sea trout estuaries in Scotland the Ythan, considers it to be one of his best lures.

The dressing is as follows:—

Our first sketch has a tail of golden pheasant tippet fibres in place and lengths of gold flat tinsel and gold coloured wool hanging. In No. 2 the wool has been wound and with the next drawing the tinsel has been put on and

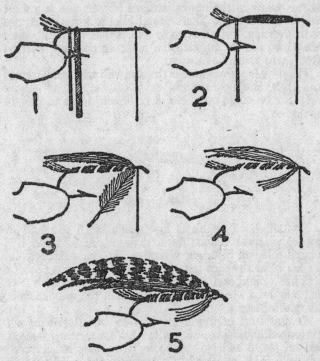

Teal and gold lure

a small bunch of bright yellow coloured deer hair is tied in and a bright yellow hackle is waiting to be wound. This has been done in No. 4 and we have the finished lure in No. 5, with its long strips of teal extending over the bend of the hook by about an inch. Depending on the water to be fished the hooks can range from No. 6 to No. 12.

Buzzer Nymph

On still water this nymph is one of the most used, it has accounted for some very big brown and rainbow trout and, like so many of the newer patterns now in use, is a most simple one to dress. There are at least a dozen variations in its dressing, but all seem to find favour with still water fish. However, its simplicity in make-up does not warrant sketches to assist the amateur.

The dressing given here is the one with which my friends and I have had most success.

It can be made on a No. 8 or down in size to No. 14 hooks.

Buzzer nymph

No tail; hook shank is first wound with fine lead or copper wire as a foundation to make it sink and over it is wound a length of bright yellow wool to near the eye. On the hook shank space left, three strands of bronze peacock herl are wound and on top of this is tied a small tuft of white or bright yellow wool to represent the wing-cases of the natural insect.

At that start of describing how to dress this nymph I mentioned hook sizes, but while I have seen many buzzers tied on No. 8 and No. 10 hooks it must be remembered this artificial is supposed to represent the pupa of a midge insect of which there are many species and all are small. However, while I have taken many trout on the large sizes my preference is for No. 14 hooks. The fly is shown in the accompanying drawing.

Baby Doll

Like the previous pattern this is a most simple one to create. It is composed entirely of wool, usually white in colour. It is essentially a still-water lure and the hooks are all long-shanked, ranging in size from No. 6 to No. 12. The more brilliant the wool is, the better its luring quality, and the sort I use is called 'Sirdar' brand.

Baby doll

You will need four strands of wool, two to form the back of the lure and tail and two for creating the body. The first pair are tied in, leaving about half-an-inch loose over the bend of the hook and, teased out, this will form the tail. The next two are tied in and wound round the shank for the body to within a quarter-of-an-inch of the eye and then tied in. The two left hanging at the tail are brought over for the back. The shank space left is filled with black floss silk and given two or three coats of black varnish. This gives it a large black head. See drawing of lure complete.

Orange Streamer

I think this pattern is an off-shoot of the Whisky Fly. Its wings, however, instead of being hackle feathers, are made of orange-dyed deer hair. It can be weighted or otherwise. For still-water I like it weighted and worked sink and draw until a new cast is needed. It is easy to make, but I emphasise once again, put some varnish on the small bunch of deer hair before tying in. If unweighted you will find that the Orange Streamer will work about a yard or four feet below the surface for some time. This is due to the buoyancy of the deer hair. After it has been in the water for several minutes it will start to slowly sink, whereas a weighted one descends straight away.

Here is the dressing with sketches to assist:—

A No. 8 long-shanked hook is used and a tail of golden

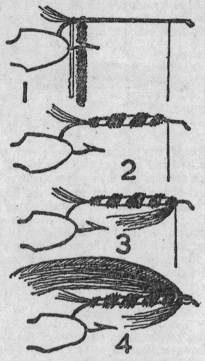

Orange streamer

pheasant topping is in position while lengths of flat gold
tinsel and bright yellow wool are waiting to be wound
round the shank. The body is complete in No. 2 with the
flat tinsel ribbing. Our next drawing has a throat hackle
of bright yellow hackle fibres. Our last sketch shows the
finished fly with a golden pheasant topping feather on top
of the deer hair.

Besides large trout this pattern has lured many salmon
and sea trout so it is one worth having as a change fly.

Golden Olive Nymph

This pattern is most useful on chalk streams and some still waters. On the Rivers Test, Itchen and other such waters in the counties of Hampshire and Dorset it is very well thought of as a killer of large trout during June and July. The nymph here described, however, differs a little from the original invented many years ago in that it has a guinea fowl wing-case. This has been proved to attract much better than the old-time starling feather wing-case.

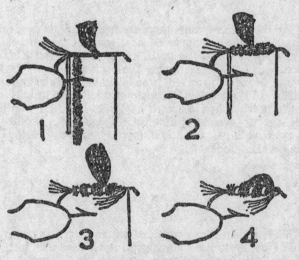

Golden olive nymph

The first sketch has a tail of grey-coloured hackle fibres in place and hanging ready to form the body are lengths of fine gauge flat gold tinsel and gold-olive coloured wool or seal's hair. Half-way along the shank there have been tied in two narrow strips of guinea fowl from a well-marked wing feather.

With No. 2 we have the wool body in position, while in the following sketch the tinsel has ribbed the wool and a throat hackle of grey fibres, similar to the tail, has been tied. With the last drawing we see the complete nymph with the guinea fowl strips brought over and tied in. The tying silk is yellow and the head is finished with clear varnish. Hooks No. 12, 14 or 16.

Stick Fly

Like the buzzer nymph there are many variations of this pattern, but the one described here is about the most easy of all flies to dress. The tail is composed of short Rhode Island Red cock hackle fibres. The back of the fly is made from a broad strip taken from a mallard drake bronze feather, and the body is constructed of four strands of bronze peacock herl. There is no throat hackle. It can be weighted or dressed ordinarily to sink very slowly. I always have a pair of each in my box, dressed on No. 12 long-shanked hooks.

Gay's Grub

This is an American weighted pattern that has recently made a name for itself among still-water fishermen in this country. The hooks generally used are No. 10 or No. 12 long-shanked.

The foundation to make it sink rapidly is fine lead or copper wire. There is no tail. A white or badger cock hackle feather is tied in near the hook bend and then a length of cream or pale yellow wool. The badger hackle is then wound to rib the wool in the same way as you would

Gay's grub

if ribbing with tinsel. The protruding feather fibres are then cut so that they look like our old friend a woolly caterpillar. It is a lure that is most useful worked, sink and draw, during June, July and August.

Dambuster

Like so many new, or should I say so-called new flies, this is just a variation of our old friend the Worm Fly, but it is a variation that has proved a winner on many still-waters throughout the country, and is a pattern I am never without when casting on such waters.

It is dressed on a No. 8, 10 or 12 long-shanked hook depending on the state of the water. For coloured water following a storm No. 8 will be found much better than the others, while for ordinary conditions No. 10 would be most suitable. For very clear water the No. 12 could prove more successful than the pair already named. So bearing

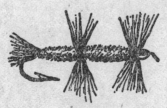

Dambuster

this in mind it is best to dress the Dambuster in the three sizes.

The tail tag is of fluorescent yellow wool, known in the tackle trade as 'D.F.' wool and can be purchased at most tackle shops. The first half of the body is four strands of bronze peacock herl, followed by a cock hackle of Rhode Island Red, which is wound like you would a dry fly. This is followed by another four strands of peacock herl, followed by another Rhode Island cock hackle. The head is black varnish.

Reason for its unusual name is that the stiff cock hackles enables the lure to move quite easily over rocks and sunken dam walls. My verdict for what it is worth: 'A most excellent pattern.'

All that remains for me to say now is 'GOOD LUCK WITH YOUR FLY DRESSING.'

OUR PUBLISHING POLICY

HOW WE CHOOSE

Our policy is to consider every deserving manuscript and we can
give special editorial help where an author is an authority on his
subject but an inexperienced writer. We are rigorously selective in
the choice of books we publish. We set the highest standards of
editorial quality and accuracy. This means that a *Paperfront* is easy
to understand and delightful to read. Where illustrations are necessary to convey points of detail, these are drawn up by a subject
specialist artist from our panel.

HOW WE KEEP PRICES LOW

We aim for the big seller. This enables us to order enormous print
runs and achieve the lowest price for you. Unfortunately, this
means that you will not find in the *Paperfront* list any titles on
obscure subjects of minority interest only. These could not be
printed in large enough quantities to be sold for the low price at
which we offer this series.
We sell almost all our *Paperfronts* at the same unit price. This
saves a lot of fiddling about in our clerical departments and helps
us to give you world-beating value. Under this system, the longer
titles are offered at a price which we believe to be unmatched by
any publisher in the world.

OUR DISTRIBUTION SYSTEM

Because of the competitive price, and the rapid turnover, *Paperfronts* are possibly the most profitable line a bookseller can handle.
They are stocked by the best bookshops all over the world. It may
be that your bookseller has run out of stock of a particular title. If
so, he can order more from us at any time—we have a fine reputa-
tion for "same day" despatch, and we supply any order, however
small (even a single copy), to any bookseller who has an account
with us. We prefer you to buy from your bookseller, as this
reminds him of the strong underlying public demand for *Paperfronts*. Members of the public who live in remote places, or who
are housebound, or whose local bookseller is unco-operative, can
order direct from us by post.

FREE

If you would like an up-to-date list of all paperfront titles cur-
rently available, send a stamped self-addressed envelope to
ELLIOT RIGHT WAY BOOKS, BRIGHTON RD.,
LOWER KINGSWOOD, SURREY, U.K